"In *Blood Brothers*, Abuna Elias Chacour took us on a journey of love in the face of oppression that was geographical, historical and personal. In *The Sermon on The Mount*, written in the cave of pandemic, Abuna invites to go even deeper by leading us out and into the blessings given on the Mount of Beatitudes. Chacour exposes his core ethic to us—a costly grace, born of deep introspection. His timely teaching gives us examples of hope, and shows us the ways we can, together, face the urgent global reality of the need for the brave, sacred, Christ-filled bonds of true peacemaking."

—Anne Weirich, president of the board, Pilgrims of I'billin

"What are a Christian's credentials? For Elias Chacour they are the nine Beatitudes and the Sermon on the Mount. This book is more about self-examination than about examining three chapters in Matthew. It challenges us to consider our prayer and fasting, to think about our confrontations with scribes and Pharisees. Above all, it asks, do we live like we truly believe that every human being is created in the image of God and worthy of dignity and respect?"

—Robert E. Sawyer, former executive director,
   Pilgrims of I'billin

"If the Sermon on the Mount is the life program of the Christian and the Beatitudes our credentials, Chacour's faithfulness as a disciple of Christ gives him ample room to challenge his readers and reflect on the Sermon on the Mount as a practice of daily living. Readers will find themselves newly invited to live more and more into the call of Jesus through his most central teaching and Chacour's witness as 'living stone.'"

—Peter J. M. Henry, minister of Word and Sacrament,
   Presbyterian Church USA

THE SERMON ON THE MOUNT

The Sermon on the Mount

*An Invitation to Receive and Advance
the Reign of God—Then, Across Time, and Now*

ELIAS CHACOUR

Edited by Duncan S. Ferguson
Foreword by Boutros Mouallem

WIPF & STOCK · Eugene, Oregon

THE SERMON ON THE MOUNT
An Invitation to Receive and Advance the Reign of God—Then, Across Time, and Now

Copyright © 2025 Elias Chacour. All rights reserved. Except for brief quotations in critical publications or reviews, no part of this book may be reproduced in any manner without prior written permission from the publisher. Write: Permissions, Wipf and Stock Publishers, 199 W. 8th Ave., Suite 3, Eugene, OR 97401.

Wipf & Stock
An Imprint of Wipf and Stock Publishers
199 W. 8th Ave., Suite 3
Eugene, OR 97401

www.wipfandstock.com

PAPERBACK ISBN: 979-8-3852-4003-6
HARDCOVER ISBN: 979-8-3852-4004-3
EBOOK ISBN: 979-8-3852-4005-0

Unless otherwise noted, scripture translations are paraphrased from the author's use of the Revised Standard Version, the New Revised Standard Version, and the Catholic Edition of the Revised Standard Version of the Bible, copyright © 1965, 1966 National Council of the Churches of Christ in the United States of America. Used by permission. All rights reserved worldwide.

Dedication
Abuna Elias Chacour

Contents

Foreword by Boutros Mouallem ix
Preface and Acknowledgments xi

CHAPTER ONE: Reflections on the Will of God 1

CHAPTER TWO: The Sermon on the Mount:
　The Life Calling of the Christian 13

CHAPTER THREE: The Companions and Conversations
　of Jesus 33

CHAPTER FOUR: On Living the Teachings of the Sermon
　on the Mount 57

CHAPTER FIVE: The Sermon on the Mount:
　The Pathway to God 74

Discussion Questions 94

Bibliography 97

Foreword

This Book Is "Something Else" and So Is Its Author

WHAT IS IN THIS book is neither a systematic study nor an academic presentation but rather "an accumulation of personal reflections" on what is called "the Sermon on the Mount." Its writer did not adduce it only as it was written in the Bible or as the philosophers, poets, and artists imagined it. No, he understood it as the "credentials" for every Christian who builds his or her credibility in this world by adhering to it.

The "Sermon on the Mount" is not just moral or social principles. It is Jesus Christ himself, the Word of God, incarnated as a human being by the Holy Spirit and the Virgin Mary. He is the Lord, the Creator of heaven and earth, immortal in the church, and the one who will come to judge the living and the dead. This Jesus is the living sermon in every line and page of the Sermon on the Mount, through teachings, proverbs, and spectacular miracles, not far, as they crowd around him.

This is the "something else" book. As for its "something else" author, no matter how he attempted to conceal himself out of modesty, he suddenly appears, merely via gaps, through a window or station from that same Sermon on the Mount, which he wants as "credentials". He tries, despite shortcomings or mistakes, to live as much as he can in his ordinary, priestly, and episcopal life. We live with him, from his childhood days in Kafr Birim, in the story or adventure of the relationship with ecclesiastical authority or the civil one with his responsibility for the "Mar Elias Educational

Institutions" and its branches or in situations of boldness and heroic confrontation, combined with humility, meekness, and tenderness.

That said, his lamp or lantern is not one to place under the bowl in the lighthouse; rather, it is that ember from the One who said, "I am the light of the world" embodied in the "Sermon on the Mount."

Archbishop Boutros Mouallem,
Archbishop Emeritus of Acre, Haifa, Nazareth, and the Rest of Galilee.

Preface and Acknowledgements

A PRAYER AND CALL FOR MERCY

My prayer: *You, O God, are the source of giving and the dispenser of wisdom. You are the first and the last. We thank you for your inspiration and guidance.*

And for you, dear reader, please do not expect perfection in this book. First, perfection belongs to God alone, and second, I did not so much seek perfection in my writing, but rather, I chose to present some of my reflections and conclusions on the Sermon on the Mount, offer them to you, and pray that they may be helpful, though perhaps incomplete. They do come from my heart!

These many and varied reflections are but a trickle of my thoughts, yet they bear a faithful witness to you, the reader, that I follow the life of the Lord, glory be to him. If you look closely at them, you will find in many places a kind of aspiration for more and a longing for something deeper. This is the essence of what is stated in this book. I do hope that you will continue the reflections, drawing upon your own faith and in your hope for the future.

Perhaps I should have added a few questions at the end of each reflection and chapter so that it becomes an invitation for you to go deeper into your experience and perhaps to add what is lacking in your own treasure of insights.[1] I wish that I could be with every reader and to learn from each one. But it is not possible,

---

1. There are some questions for discussion and reflection at the end of the book.

Preface and Acknowledgements

and I call on you, the reader, to contribute through your witness and complete what is lacking in the witness of your brother, Abuna Elias Chacour.

I want these thoughts and reflections to be a motivation for you, the reader, to contribute your wisdom to the problems we face. Together, we can expand the reign of God with our commitment to love and justice. So, with your deep faith and your wisdom, please pursue the message of these pages and continue to be a witness to the One who loved and continues to love our troubled world and all those in it.

A POINT OF VIEW AND AN EXPRESSION OF GRATITUDE

In Genesis, we read that God created man and woman, and that God said, "This is very good," meaning that God created them together in the divine image and likeness. The implication of this account is that we are all created by God with the capacity to understand our responsibilities to love him in return and follow the will of God across the years of our lives. The passage also suggests that no one has the right to claim perfection or superiority, nor does anyone have the right to claim exclusive wisdom or a higher priority. Rather, we all must humble ourselves and acknowledge that we were created in the image of God, that is, with the capacity to understand and live together in the bond of love. We are compatible, complementing each other, and called to love those in need. Likewise, when you read these reflections, they need your response and your constructive vision on how to create a more just and humane world.

And we then ask, are we not all members of one creation of the human family with one purpose, and for those of us in the Christian family, are we not one body, which is the body of Christ? The Lord Jesus, glory be to him, said: "Who are you to judge someone else's servant? . . . You, follow me."[2] Following Christ means

---

2. See Matt 25:14–30.

Preface and Acknowledgements

dealing with everyone with a loving heart and at times turning a blind eye to the weakness of others. Our calling is to thank God for our brothers and sisters and then to make our contribution to spreading the faith. We are partners in working in the Lord's field. I welcome you and invite your contribution in this field of life.

It is my duty to extend my thanks and appreciation to our son, the son of Birim, in fact the son of our institutions where he got his start, and Professor Jeries Makhoul, who spared no effort and did not skimp on time in reading and reviewing the manuscript, refining its language, and amending its wording as he saw fit. May God reward him. He was patient and cheerful during all stages of reading the manuscript. There are no words which I have that will give due justice to his contribution. I leave it to God to bless him, his family, and his children. This was his first mission with us, in this field, and he was generous with his scholarship, knowledge, and faith. Our wish and prayer are that the coming ministries will be greater and more abundant than the past ones. I want to thank as well my colleague Khaled Farah who translated the manuscript into English, no small task and one for which I am profoundly grateful.

My secretary, the honorable Mrs. Nasreen Halloun, deserves our sincere thanks and deep appreciation for her well-known patience and perseverance in printing the manuscript, tabulating it, and following up on every detail. She deserves her reward from God Almighty; protect her health, her husband, her two sons and her family, and may success and good fortune come to her forever. She has been a faithful and patient partner in the completion of this book the entire way. I bear witness to her goodness through my deep love and appreciation.

There are many whom God placed on my path, and they have provided advice, an idea, or a suggestion that enriched this work. They all have my thanks and appreciation from the heart. They know that my message, since I began, has been shared with many from around the world. These people, our friends in Germany and all European countries, and in the United States and Australia, have the credit for encouraging the publication of this book. Thus, the message in its pages is in response to their wishes that I write down some of my thoughts about the Sermon on the Mount. They have, in many projects and in many situations, encouraged us, accompanied us in our achievements, and believed in the path we are taking. May God bless them and shower them with blessings and peace. I can only hope that what is contained in this book will be helpful and encouraging to their faith.

I give my thanks to my dear friend, Duncan Ferguson, a scholar, minister, and teacher, who has consented to assist me in expressing myself well in English, not my first language. For example, I have given him permission to be careful about using the masculine "he" as a reference to God, knowing that God does not have a gender and there is the risk that we will understand God from a dominant masculine frame of reference. There may be times when it is wise to allow the reference to God as Father; it has been an expression of comfort in my years of understanding God as a loving Parent, and therefore I often use "God the Father" in my conversations and writing. On occasion, the masculine reference to God is part of my pattern of speaking and the structure of my writing in that it communicates that God does love us, not unlike a parent's pure and unconditional love for a child. But in no way do I want to be exclusive or diminish the understanding of God by the occasional use of the masculine "Father" or "he." God is equally feminine and a loving Mother.

A final word of thanks to everyone who has accompanied me in prayer. I want to convey to everyone the greatness of what God has done for Elias Chacour, faithful servant of God. God the Creator raised this humble servant, satisfied him with a hunger for goodness, and quenched his thirst for righteousness.

Your brother,
Archbishop Elias Chacour
Archbishop Emeritus of Acre, Haifa, Nazareth, and the Rest of Galilee

CHAPTER ONE

Reflections on the Will of God

Blessed are the pure in heart, for they will see God.

(MATT 5:8)

WHAT IS CONTAINED IN this book is not a systematic study nor an academic presentation, but rather an accumulation of reflections about our troubled world and the way we respond in compassion to it. Finding my way became the essence of my independent and personal studies of the Sermon on the Mount as contained in the Gospel of Matthew, chapters 5–7. On occasion, there are also reflections on the texts of all four Gospels, the Acts of the Apostles, the Epistles of Paul, and the book of Revelation. They are the contemplations of the demanding life of a bishop resulting from his retreats, prayers, and reflections on the life of the Savior. The dominant element is the constant admiration for the life and personality of the One born of Mary, Jesus, who has given us life through his miracles and teachings. It is as though the author is swimming in the ocean of God's love, in the abundance of divine generosity, in the overflow of God's Spirit, and in the presence of all who believe in God and follow God in all the stages of life that lead to salvation.[1]

---

1. One may also need to reflect on the way that God's love is cosmic, going beyond life on earth.

The Sermon on the Mount

There are three main focal points in these reflections regarding the Sermon on the Mount. The first focal point is the text of the accreditation of the person from Nazareth by a group of church leaders in Nazareth:

> The Spirit of the Lord is upon me, because he has anointed me to bring good news to the poor. He has sent me to proclaim release to the captives and recovery of sight to the blind, to let the oppressed go free, to proclaim the year of the Lord's favor. (Luke 4:18–19)

The second focal point is the way that we use the expression "the kingdom of God," by which we mean the reign of God, God fully present in those people who use the Sermon on the Mount as their guide as they seek to do God's will. The use of the title "kingdom of God" will occasionally occur, but more often I will use the expression "reign of God," capturing the true meaning of the kingdom of God while avoiding the masculine reference to God as King. The reign of God is an inclusive term. Our use of the expression "the reign of God" is to say that God is present and active in the lives of believers (the people who are filled with the presence and power of God) and, indeed, present in all of reality. We do not want our understanding of God to be "too small."[2]

The third focal point regarding the Sermon on the Mount is to name the credentials of all who follow Christ on the path of salvation, and these are the nine Beatitudes. We see the life of Jesus Christ summarized in the nine Beatitudes, which we find in Matt 5:3–12:

> Blessed are the poor in spirit, for theirs is the kingdom of heaven.
>
> Blessed are the meek, for they will inherit the earth.
>
> Blessed are those who mourn, for they will be comforted.
>
> Blessed are those who hunger and thirst for righteousness, for they will be filled.
>
> Blessed are the merciful, for they will be shown mercy.

---

2. See Phillips, *Your God Is Too Small*.

Blessed are the pure in heart, for they will see God.

Blessed are the peacemakers, for they will be called children of God.

Blessed are you when they curse you, persecute you, and slander you falsely, in my Name.

Rejoice and be glad, because great is your reward in heaven, for in this same way they have persecuted the prophets who were before you.

Those who leave everything and follow Christ in all aspects of their lives and give themselves to loving others have the Beatitudes as credentials. We find the details of how to live the Christian life in the Sermon on the Mount, following the Beatitudes in the Gospel of Matthew, chapters 5, 6, and 7. We make them our map for life as we give ourselves to God and seek to understand fully what it means to do God's will and follow God's way.

"I am Who I am, I am He." This is what the Creator said to the prophet Moses in front of the burning bush. This is what Jesus Christ reiterated repeatedly in pivotal situations. "I am He!" is a name chosen by the God who appeared to Moses, and the son of Nazareth says, "I am He!," the same one who appeared to Moses in the bush and revealed to him the divine name: "I am He! I AM!" (Exod 3:1–15).

We sanctify the name of God as we pray, "Hallowed be thy Name," which means venerating the "Name" (God). Here we can note a truth which Jesus Christ revealed to us during his life on earth, especially in the Sermon on the Mount: we have a loving God in heaven who knows everything, cares about everything, and blesses everything and everyone. We perform acts of goodness in God's name, respecting the divine presence among us. When we pray, we must turn to God and humbly acknowledge that we are servants of God.

In order to remain fully in God's presence, we must fast, honor God by giving alms, and then forgive, respect, and help others, just as God helps us and wants us to help one another. We are God's children and creatures whom God loves. God takes delight in us. God is our loving Father/mother and is present with and in us as the Holy Spirit, empowering us to pray and to be assured that wherever we are, God is with us.[3] We are God's children by adoption, and we have the right, by the grace of God, to be with God, even as Jesus is seated at the right hand of God. God says to us, "I want you to be where I am." God, our heavenly Parent, protects the birds of the air and the beasts of the field. God is present in the creation, which is a sign that God will protect us, the culmination of God's creation. We are God's children by adoption, and this is made possible by Jesus, who took the form of a servant so that we might attain adoption. Jesus said to his disciples, "Take heart, for I have overcome the world" (John 16:33).[4]

In the Sermon on the Mount, the Lord Christ purifies every impurity that causes us to disobey God's laws, thus restoring to us our dignity. This restoration is described often in the life of Jesus. For example, he clarifies the place of the law on several occasions. One vivid illustration is when he explains the meaning of the Sabbath as he heals a man with a disability on the Sabbath. When questioned whether this was "work," prohibited on the Sabbath, he replies that it was acceptable on the Sabbath as an act of love. To refrain from work on the Sabbath is not an artificial legal demand but a time for us to rest and restore our souls: "For the Sabbath was made for man, not man for the Sabbath" (Luke 6:6–11).

PURIFICATION STARTS FROM WITHIN

In the Sermon on the Mount, God, through Jesus, always faithful, restores the dignity and true meaning of the law. Jesus has not come to abolish the law, but rather, to fulfill it. The will of Christ, for those who follow him, is to practice true righteousness, not the artificial legalism of the so-called righteousness of the scribes and Pharisees. True purification begins from within. Therefore,

---

3. Here I have been careful not to use the term "Father," although it continues to be a natural expression for me as I feel loved by a parent.

4. It seemed appropriate not to use "Father" in these passages, although that was my initial inclination.

we must purify ourselves from the inside first and then be transformed. The murderer, for example, because this person is not transformed, may wake up in the morning and kill his brother. This is because the heart of this person has not been purified. When a person harbors evil for another person, it means that this person does not understand that humans are the "custodian" of others and must care for them. This person who kills denounces God's authority over life and death and takes the right to life in his or her own hands, going against the law of God.

The same principle applies in reference to human sexuality and marriage. "Whoever looks at a woman with lust has committed adultery with her in his heart" (Matt 5:28). The scribes taught that the *fatwa* (verdict) regarding marriage was that anyone who divorces his wife must give her a legal certificate of divorce, not unlike what one might do with a transfer of property. But Jesus and early Christian teaching reject the notion that the wife is "property," understanding her as a person of great value and one who should be treated with respect, blessing the sanctity of marriage between two human beings created in the image of God. So, Jesus teaches that "what God has joined together, let no man put asunder," because whoever divorces his wife leaves her exposed to abuse. In addition, the law taught that whoever marries an adulteress has committed adultery. In this passage (Matt 5:27–30), we note that Jesus honored women and did not see them as property that can be discarded or traded. He honors women and stands against anything that does not treat them with great respect or that will cause them harm.

Jesus understands the seriousness of adultery, and he was especially sensitive to what might be called "spiritual adultery." For example, it was taught in some of the cities Jesus and the apostle Paul visited that whoever strips himself naked before any of the idol gods (a common religious practice) is sinful. In other words, whoever gives in to the temptations of life and inclinations to evil, whoever seeks to worship anything other than God, is a person who has committed adultery. According to the law of Moses, the adulterer deserves death by stoning. Jesus was more forgiving than those who followed Moses about this law but very clear about the foundational value of faithful trust in marriage.

Jesus took a stand against the scribes who distorted the law of God and substituted their own teachings for it by accepting the principle of "the justice of revenge." This practice was an accepted norm, and people did believe in the notion of "an eye for an eye and a tooth for a tooth." But he, that is Christ, says to us: Resist the Evil One, and do not repeat the "judge and straighten" system, or the "get even" practice. Rather, love your enemies, bless those who curse you, do good unto those from whom you do not expect good in return. Freely you have received, so freely give. As for you, forgive your brother and your sister seventy times seven.

It is sometimes difficult for us to believe how dangerous paganism and its practices were in the time of Jesus. When he was incarnated and came to us, he enlightened us about the practices of the time that went against the will of God. The lights came on! He came to confirm the truth that all who follow God have the sacred duty to love others. It is our sacred responsibility to love our enemies and pray for them.

Similarly, the Lord, glory be to him, teaches us to give charitably without being concerned about people seeing us do it. In order to ensure that people do not see us giving charity, we give our offering in secret. Neither the pagan nor the believer should know. Then, our loving God, who sees and understands, rewards us. Jesus Christ teaches us that our charity should be in secret: "Do not let your left hand know what your right hand has done, but your Father who sees in secret will reward you" (Matt 6:3). This is especially the case in our charity, whatever it may be, and it is an integral part of God's generosity to honor the good we do.

When we give alms, we should not ask God to increase the number of the needy in order to show how great our compassion is for them. Rather, we give alms to help relieve the distress of the needy, and we pray for them and have compassion for our brother and sister in need. We do not pray that God increase the number of poor and needy people so that we can give alms to them and feel righteous. Rather, we give alms and pray that the needy will be able to find ways to be self-sufficient. We should thank those who accept our charity as a gift, from one person to another, allowing us both to share in God's bounties.

We pray willingly; the Lord does not force us to pray but tells us instead that when you pray, go into your room, close your door, and pray to your heavenly Parent who loves you. Do not speak at length during your prayer, for it is not by chatter that our prayers will be answered, especially since we have a loving God in heaven who knows all of our needs. God provides for the birds in the sky and the wild animals in the forest. Will God not also provide for us as children in need?

The same principle applies to prayer. Jesus teaches us:

> When you pray, pray like this:
> Our Father in heaven
> Hallowed be your Name
> Your kingdom come,
> Your will be done
> on earth as it is in heaven . . . (Matt 6:9–13)

It is by praying this prayer that we honor God's reign and God's power and glory. The words "our Father" and not "my Father" mean that we pray in the name of all people, addressing the One who loves everyone.[5] How dare we seek evil for others and not good when the God of love in heaven says to us, speaking through Jesus Christ, "If you do not forgive people for their transgressions, then your heavenly Father will not forgive your own transgressions!" This becomes our stepping stone towards being faithful and fasting (the act of renewal and purification), expressing our loving relationship with God. It is not for exhibition in front of people, nor for people to praise us or reward us for our fasting.

As Jesus closes this part of his teaching to the disciples, he urges them to store up for themselves treasures in heaven, not on earth, and to enter through the narrow gate, not through the wide gate through which many seek to enter into God's presence. He teaches his followers to lay up for themselves treasures in heaven,

---

5. Once again, we leave the prayer addressed to "Father," which would have been easily understood in his time as the one who provides.

where no moth ravages and no thief steals. Seek first the reign of God and God's righteousness, and all that we need will be given to us.

THE GOLDEN RULE

In the seventh chapter of the Gospel of Matthew, from the Sermon on the Mount, the Lord reassures his disciples that God will provide us with what we need. Then, approaching the end of his teaching, he tells them that they should understand the quintessence of the law in these words: "So in everything, do to others what you would have them do to you" (Matt 7:12). This, he says, is the meaning of the law and the prophets. The fate of not following this teaching in times of distress is the fate of the house built on sand, which collapses in a storm, but the house built on rock is unshakable, for it is stronger than any storm.

We learn from the Sermon on the Mount that we are not saved through speech or a multitude of words but by brief and basic speech, focusing on what the most important subject is which we want to express. He concludes with a reminder to be simple and sincere in your prayers, so "let your words be 'Yes, Yes,' or 'No, No'; anything more than this comes from the evil one" (Matt 5:37).

At the end of the Sermon on the Mount, we see the scribes troubled by Jesus and his teaching, perhaps envious and devising a plan to get rid of this one who says that he came from God and to God he will return. But the blessed people, when they came to hear the words of Jesus, were amazed at his teachings because he was teaching them as one who had authority, not as their scribes. We, the priests and ministers of Christ and the missionaries called to spread his teachings, must focus on enabling the people to know the person of Jesus.

Jesus goes on to teach that pastors and teachers must learn how best to preach and teach the many people who come to listen. Those with these responsibilities need to evaluate the response of the congregation after the sermon or lesson that was delivered on Sunday and their teaching on other occasions. Do people leave the church impressed by what the priest or pastor elucidated, and then are they lifted out of their isolation and doubt, thanking God for saving them from falling? Or is there just boredom during the sermon? Do they then say, "Maybe next Sunday, God willing? But there is nothing for me now"? This is often what happens when the people hear the priest's words in the sermon. It becomes either a light that shines in the church which leads to heaven or the hollow words that lead nowhere.

The Sermon on the Mount begins with the disciples surrounding the divine Teacher and ends with the crowds enjoying and listening to what the Teacher says: "And when Jesus had finished these words, the crowds were amazed at his teaching, because he taught them as one who had authority, and not as their scribes" (Matt 7:28). What is the reaction of those who believe in him? What is our reaction to what we have heard? Is it admiration and a willingness to follow the way of God? Which "seeds" fall into the ground: those which do not bear fruit, or those which do bear fruit? Are we the ones whose words fall on the road, or the ones whose seeds fall on the sidewalk, or the ones whose seeds fall in the ground that is full of deadly thorns, or the ones whose seeds fall, by the grace of God, on the good soil? What fruits do we bear and in what quantity? Do we carry thirty, sixty, or a hundred grains of wheat? What matters is that the words of the Teacher must express the love of God.

Our deeds are our answer, and the day of harvest determines our yield and its quantity. Some may think that the teachings of Jesus in the Sermon on the Mount are difficult and hard to understand and apply, and then they may look for an alternative message and pathway that widens the entrance gate. The Savior, glory be to him, tells us: "Enter through the narrow gate." Few people try to enter through it, unlike the wide door. But the narrow gate leads to salvation while the wide gate leads to ruin. One enters the kingdom of heaven (reign of God) through hard struggle, and those who do receive its benefits are few. Jesus says that "not everyone who says to me: 'Lord, Lord,' will enter the kingdom of heaven. But whoever takes up his cross and follows me will enter the kingdom" (Mark 8:34–37).

The Sermon on the Mount, in all of its details, was not primarily delivered for us to admire its beauty nor even the depth of its content. Rather, it is there for us to follow and to live by its teaching. Faith is not so much a matter of admiration for the teacher but rather a matter of dedication and witness. Just as Christ lived as a perfect model in Nazareth, so those who follow Christ must seek to have his faith and righteousness. Our dedication must surpass the righteousness of the Sadducees and the scribes. As Jesus did, so we must follow the Beatitudes. He who has ears to hear, let him or her hear.

In order for us to understand the Sermon on the Mount and the message of Jesus Christ and make their message the program of our lives, we must understand the three chapters in Matthew's Gospel which constitute the Sermon on the Mount. As we do, it is necessary to read what comes before it and after it in order to fully understand Christ's message and have a grasp of the Gospel of Matthew in which the sermon is present. As we read and pray, we will begin to grasp that Jesus is the expression of the perfection of the law and the prophets, the One to hear and follow.

The Gospel of Matthew was written several years after the events and the teaching it records, about AD 90. It is perhaps the union of two documents: the Gospel of Mark and the wisdom found in an accumulation of documents referred to as Q (source). It has three main sections: the figure of Jesus as the Messiah, his public ministry that included Israel's repudiation of him, and the account of the end of his life in Jerusalem by death on the cross and his resurrection. There is this marvelous account of the teaching of Jesus called the Sermon on the Mount, which we are studying. The "Mount" may be a reference to a hill on the western side of the Sea of Galilee where large groups could go and perhaps hear from the teachers of Judaism. It is thought that Jesus would speak from the hill where he could be heard. What we have in the Gospel of Matthew is an exceptional summary of his teaching, called the Sermon on the Mount, collections of what people heard him say and then passed on to others in an oral tradition. This Sermon on the Mount is the subject of our study, including some sections that are very well known such as the Beatitudes, the Lord's Prayer, and the golden rule that we should treat others as we want to be treated.

CHRIST IS THE FULFILLMENT OF THE PROPHECIES AND THE PROPHETS

Jesus did not heal all of the sick nor did he cleanse all the lepers. He did not open the eyes of all the blind, and he did not raise all of the dead. He healed some, cleansed some, and opened the eyes of some in fulfillment of the prophecy of Isaiah, describing the messiah who opens the door of hope for all, and blessed are those who have faith in him. He bore our transgressions and took upon himself our sins, and he became our redemption. He also demolished the wall separating the nations. There is no longer Jew or gentile (foreigner), no difference between a man and a woman, and no distinction between a master and a slave, as we have all been called to become children of God by adoption. The door became open for anyone who carries a disability, illness, or human frailty, enabling us to unite with the suffering of Christ and to wear the garment of salvation. Everyone who extends a helping hand to the sick or the needy has become as one who is extending a helping hand to the Savior, Jesus Christ.

Our diseases, infirmities, and mistakes have a healing dimension for us and others; they give us empathy! I urge all believers to read the Sermon on the Mount and internalize it. It has been given to you, and to everyone who was born a child in the image and likeness of God, to live the message of the Sermon in life. May the grace of our Lord God and our Savior Jesus Christ be with you and in your hearts. Amen.

> "And, behold, I come in haste; and my reward is with me, to give every person according to the merit of their deeds. I am the Alpha and the Omega, the beginning and the end, the first and the last. Blessed are those who wash

their robes, so that they may have the right to the tree of life and that they may enter the city by the gates. I, Jesus, have sent my angel to testify unto you these things in the churches. I am the Root and the Offspring of David, and the bright Morning Star." Amen. Come, O Lord Jesus. (Rev 21:1–8)

The grace of the Lord Jesus be with you.

CHAPTER TWO

The Sermon on the Mount: The Life Program of the Christian

"You are the salt of the earth... You are the light of the world."

(MATT 5:13A–14A)

WE ENGAGE IN THE study of the Sermon on the Mount in part because we want to understand more fully how it teaches us to live wisely and well in the challenging conditions in which we find ourselves. We live in perilous times! For example, I write at the time of the election of the president of the United States. As I inform myself about the implications of the selection of a new president, I realize how important this decision is for those in the United States, and even for those who live in Israel/Palestine. I also realize that it is important for most of those from other countries as well given that the United States does have an influence around the world.

My Christian faith teaches me to use my life, even in a small way, to improve the lives of others, and I do so in a dangerous world; it is there even in the fine print in the election of the new president of the United States. The expression of love is the hallmark of the Christian, and each of us has ways of expressing love and concern for those who suffer. Yet we may not have adequate resources to manage the demands of contemporary life. I do feel called to understand better the Sermon on the Mount as a foundational document that teaches us how we might invest time and energy in reducing human suffering and to give ourselves to the creation of a more just and humane world.

THE CREDENTIALS AND CONTEXT OF THE TEACHING OF JESUS

The Sermon on the Mount is a comprehensive description of the Christian way of life and describes the values which are the foundation of the Christian journey across the span of life. The nature of this journey begins in Matt 5:3–12 with the Beatitudes, which may be thought of as the *credentials* of the Christian. They express the values, attitudes, and spirit of every Christian who seeks to follow Christ and walk in his footsteps. This means that the Christian is one who may even be called to carry the cross and follow Christ. The essential content of the Beatitudes is the pathway of being Christian.

The Beatitudes assume that the Christian has had a conversion and seeks to understand what follows from the initial commitment to follow Christ. The new Christian soon discovers that the conversion leads to purification or a deep and fundamental change of the way one travels through life. Initially, it may feel overwhelming, but new Christians soon discover that they now have the empowering presence of God's Spirit, enabling them to live maturely and follow the will of God. Of course, there are many dimensions to the will of God, but the initial direction for the new Christian is to live in harmony with the *nomos*, meaning God's laws, which are instructions on how we are to live. All Christians have the example of Jesus, the one who lived life with great integrity in following the will and way of God.

Christ's credentials are found in the reading of Isaiah in the Nazareth synagogue, where we read: "The Spirit of the Lord is upon me, because God has anointed me to preach the good news to the poor, and has sent me to announce to the captives their freedom, and to the blind the restoration of their sight, and to relieve the oppressed, and proclaim a year of the Lord's favor" (Luke 4:18–21). These verses speak of the coming of a jubilee year, one in which the debts we owe to others are forgiven and in which people get their fields back which have been used as security for a debt. At the end of reading these credentials, Jesus stands in front of the synagogue assembly and solemnly announces: "Today, these verses you have heard have been fulfilled."

THE CHRISTIAN'S CREDENTIALS

The Christian's credentials are the nine Beatitudes. They express the foundational values of the Christian and describe what it means to be disciple and follow Christ. We learn about being a disciple in the Sermon on the Mount, chapters 5–7 in Saint Matthew's Gospel. Jesus says, "I have not come to abolish the law; but rather to fulfill it," reassuring those Jewish listeners that he is not discounting the law but speaking about its full content, both in attitude and behavior (Matt 5:17).

The challenge for new Christians is that they must interact with the world, and the world will inevitably influence them. True Christians exist in the world, but they are not of this world and will therefore need guidance. They do not have an everlasting city on earth where there are no challenges. Nor should they store up treasures for themselves on earth; rather, they have treasures in heaven. The true Christian, then, is one who walks, endorses, and receives the reign of God; the empowering grace of God fills them. New Christians are able to say in their heart, "Thy will be done, O Lord, as it is in heaven, also on earth."

The life of the Christian is to carry the cross, which the world does not accept; the cross takes the form of loving one's enemies, praying for the persecuted, fasting in secret, being generous to the needy, and visiting the sick. The Christian follows Christ and is constantly aware that his or her life is heading towards the resurrection, although the new Christian should not underestimate the reality of suffering, nor should they doubt the reality of the resurrection. This is the Christian's path towards the loving God, who tends to every human being and every creature with care and love. There is forgiveness for the sinner and divine mercy for the guilty. God does not coexist with sin but removes it. The merciful God hates harmful and sinful behavior and revives the sinner, cleanses the sinner, and restores the sinner's purity.

THE CHRISTIAN'S CONFRONTATION WITH THE SCRIBES AND PHARISEES

As we read this Sermon, we look at ourselves as Christ did, confronting the modern day "scribes and Pharisees" regarding the teachings that should guide our lives. In other words, we are on a journey not unlike that of Jesus. We are in a search of salvation, grateful for who we are and where we are going, understanding that it is a journey that we travel with God and that we must always honor that relationship. Therefore, our fasting, for example, should be a joy in front of people because we are in communion with God and discipline ourselves to be faithful. We must remember that God knows everything about us; God is our Creator and loves us as a parent. God, then, does not act like a secular ruler or judge, but rather, the one who has mercy upon us and who leads us to the paradise of peace and happiness. We join with God and seek to do God's will in the world. We are called to have mercy upon those who suffer, the one lying in front of our house covered with sores while dogs lick them. We must not harden our hearts and close our eyes as we pass this person but go with God's blessing to heal this person and reduce human suffering.

In this context, I remember a story of a man walking with a bucket in each hand, one full of water and the other full of fire. Those who passed by asked him, "Why are you carrying these two buckets? What will you do with them?" He replied, "With one bucket, I will be light in the heavens, and with the other, I will drown in hell!" Humans were created by God to carry the bucket of life and follow the will and way of God. We must not carry any bucket of destruction. We must wipe every tear from every eye and be a smile of hope for everyone.

WE LIVE TO REVEAL THE GLORY OF GOD THROUGH OUR ACTIONS

We do not live our Christian life for its own sake; rather, we live it for the glory of God in the service of humanity. Yet there is a reward, and the Beatitudes end with the reward: "Your heavenly Father/mother will reward you" (Matt 6:4). If you live the Beatitudes, you will know God and become children of God. It is a reward that comes from our holiness. The expectation of reward is not a bad thing but rather a good thing if our ultimate goal is the glory of God expressed in the living person who seeks to do God's will. We may be unsure where our reward may come from, perhaps either from God or from people. But Jesus is clear: our reward comes from God. We may lack full understanding, as Jesus teaches: "Your right hand does not know what your left hand is doing." So it is your heavenly Parent who will reward you. If the preacher is only concerned with what people say about his preaching, then he will receive the reward from people, and nothing remains for him to expect from God. And you, dear preacher, may have received your reward in your life from people, but the true reward comes from God.

Jesus teaches: "When you give charity, do not let your right hand know what your left is doing, and when you fast, do not go around looking miserable, like the hypocrites who wash their face and groom themselves so as not to show to the people that you are fasting, but God, who sees in secret, will reward you openly" (Matt 6:1–4). God is the judge. God brings together everything, all of our deeds until the day when the books are opened and people are held accountable for their deeds. We are held accountable for everything we have done on earth, and for everything we did in secret, God rewards us openly. We can hide what we do from people, but we cannot hide anything from God. If we forget everything that is earthly and do everything on earth for the glory of God

Almighty, God will record and take into account everything we have done. It is important to hear and accept what is being said in this statement: "I was in prison and you visited me, I was thirsty and you gave me something to drink" (Matt 25:36). The righteous ask, and it may have escaped their memory, "When did we see you imprisoned or thirsty and helped you?" He answers, "All things are as it is written: 'Whatever you have done in secret, I will reward you publicly.'" This is the day when the books will be opened, the day when everything hidden will be revealed, and intentions will be announced to the entire world. He also says to us, "You have done well, O good and trustworthy servant. You have been entrusted over the small amount; I will put you in charge of the large amount. Enter into the joy of your Lord" (Matt 25:21).

THE PRAYER OF CHRIST'S DISCIPLES

The Christian's prayer begins with drawing close to God, with piety and reverence, with deep humility, penitence, and true joy. We do not draw close to God by using empty words or pretending to be seen "as religious" in front of people. Getting closer to God is not a public show in order that people will see that we are spiritual. Prayer is a soliloquy with God who loves us.

> Therefore, when you pray, do not be like the hypocrites, for they choose to pray standing in synagogues and at road junctions in order to be seen by people. For verily I say to you, they have received their reward. As for you, when you pray, go into your room, lock the door, and pray in secret to your Father, who is there, and your Father, who sees in secret, will reward you.[1] And when you pray, do not speak like hypocrites, for they believe that they will be answered on account of their many words. Do not imitate them, because your Father knows what you need before you ask Him. (Matt 6:1–5)

So, pray like the prophet Elijah did on the day of the burnt offering.

---

1. Again, we use the word "Father" in that it is a good way to capture the meaning of this passage.

ELIJAH'S STRUGGLE WITH THE PROPHETS OF BAAL

There is the story in 1 Kgs 18 about what Elijah said to the prophets of Baal:

> "You call on the name of your god, and I will call on the name of the Lord, and the god who answers by fire, he is God." And all the people answered, "This is well spoken." Then Elijah said to the prophets of Baal: "Choose for yourselves one bull and you start, for you are many, and call on the name of your god, but put no fire to the bull." And they took the bull that was given them, prepared it, and called upon the name of Baal from morning until noon, saying, "O Baal, answer us!" But there was no sound, and no one answered. And they danced around the altar that was made by human hands. When noon came, Elijah mocked them, saying, "Cry aloud, for he is a god. Maybe he is busy, or he is in seclusion, or he is on a journey, or perhaps he is asleep and must be awakened." And they screamed louder and cut themselves, according to their custom, with swords and spears, until the blood dripped on them. Noon passed as they were prophesying until it was time for the offering, but there was no voice; no one answered and no one listened. The next day, Elijah said to all the people: "Come near to me." So, all the people approached him, . . . and he built an altar of stones in the name of the Lord, made of twelve stones, and made a water trench large enough to contain nine measures of grains around the altar. Then he arranged the firewood, executed the bull, and placed it on the firewood. When it was time for the offering, Elijah the Prophet came forward and said in prayer: "O Lord God of Abraham, Isaac, and Jacob, let it be known today that you are the God in Israel, and that I am your servant, and by your command, I have done all these things. Answer me, O Lord, answer me, or hear me, O Lord, hear me, so that this people may know that you, O Lord, you are God, and you have turned their hearts back." Then the fire of the Lord came down and consumed Elijah's offering and burned the wood, and removed the stones and the soil,

until it licked up the water that was in the trench. When the people saw this, they fell on their faces and said, "The Lord is God, the Lord is God." (1 Kgs 18:24–40)

This is Elijah's brief prayer, short and meaningful, without exaggeration or hypocrisy, and without meaningless words, as the prophets of Baal did before Baal, whose prayer was wordy with no life in it.

As for you, believe that God, your loving Parent, knows that you need the essentials of your human and physical life. God knows what you need, just as the father of the prodigal son knew what his son, who returned repentant to his embrace, needed. So, pray like this: "Our Father, who art in heaven." Do not say "my Father, who art in heaven." Rather, say "our Father, who art in heaven," because God is the Parent of all, indeed the loving God of all human beings and the Creator of all that exists, whether human, animal, or inanimate.[2] "God saw everything that he had made, and indeed, it was very good" (Gen 1:31a).

I believe in one God, Creator of heaven and earth. God is the God of the entire universe. God created it beautiful (*kallos*), and after God created a person, God looked at this person and said, "He/She is very good." This reminds us of the name that Greek philosophers gave to God the Creator: He was beautiful and good, that is, "*Kalós kaí agathós.*"

THE TAX COLLECTOR'S PRAYER

The prayers of the Pharisee and of the tax collector stand before our eyes as examples to teach us how Jesus Christ wants us to pray. He does not want us to be like that pharisee who entered the temple with his head held high like an empty ear of grain and prayed to God Almighty: "O God, I thank you because I am not like the rest of the infidel and corrupt people, nor like that tax collector.

---

2. Again, we are using "Father" as a way of speaking about a loving God who is like a wonderful parent.

I fast twice a week, and I pay tithes on my entire income" (Luke 18:9–12). The pharisee entered with an inflated ego, showing disdain for the tax collector, considering him so sinful that he did not dare raise his head and thinking to himself that he, the pharisee, was "righteous and innocent." He did not mention that his money was the temple's money that he had stolen.

The tax collector, however, entered the temple, trembling because he admitted that he was a sinner, so he sat or knelt behind the last seat and bowed his head, closed his eyes, and began to say in the depths of his heart, "O God, forgive me, the sinner, and have mercy on me." He did not look around, and he did not care for people to see him, for he was a sinner and was content that God saw him, for God was merciful and forgiving.

Woe to those who declare themselves innocent. The result of this person's prayer, the one approved by the Master, to whom glory be, saying, "This one returned to his home justified and with integrity." This person returned as a friend of God, and God walks with her and takes care of her. It is as if she returned to the earthly paradise, living in the company of God and keeping pace with God, that is, walking with God.

It seems to me as if the Lord feels sad for this boastful pharisee when God says, "this one," meaning the tax collector who returned home justified while "that one," the pharisee, returned unjustified. He was condemned because his prayer did not enter the heart of the Lord. Sister Mary Bewardi, my dear friend, noted in a conversation that in heaven, we find all vices forgiven and we do not find pride, and in hell, we find all virtues condemned and do not find humility.[3]

ZACCHAEUS WAS ALSO THE SON OF ABRAHAM (LUKE 19:1-10)

We need to consider how Jesus took the side of sinners so that they would return to God, and God, in turn, would receive them.

---

3. Sister Mary Bewardi, personal correspondence with author. Sister Mary Bewardi served as a missionary in the northern part of Galilee.

The Sermon on the Mount

"I came not to call the righteous, but the sinners" (Luke 5:32). We have an example in the entry of Jesus into Jericho where there was a man who was a tax collector, and he was considered by others to be a sinner, a thief, and unworthy of God's care. The Gospel of Luke tells us that he was "small in stature" and also small in status and not respected, but he had heard about Jesus and desired with all his might to see Jesus. But how could he get past all the people to have the privilege of seeing Jesus? His stature did not allow him to see over the people or get close, nor did his status allow him to compete with those of stature to reach Jesus. However, he knew where the Master was going to pass, so he climbed a large sycamore tree having branches extending out above the street through which the Master was passing. He did not wonder whether it was a noble act for a rich man like him to climb the tree. Rather, Zacchaeus climbed the tree and waited for Jesus to pass under it, with him on the branch above, so that he would see the Master and be content with that. He did not comprehend that it was not permissible for him to be higher than the Teacher, and that the Teacher would pass below under him. But Jesus knew everything, so he said to him, "I saw you when you were under the fig tree." He said to him, "Zacchaeus, hurry and come down, for I must stay at your house and eat with you." It is as if he said to Zacchaeus: "You searched for me in order to see me, and you climbed the tree, and behold, I found you. For this reason, come down from the sycamore tree and accompany me to your house. Do not climb the tree, but humble yourself as it befits you."

As soon as he approached that sycamore tree and saw that Zacchaeus had climbed up on a branch, the Teacher looked at him and said: "Zacchaeus, come down. You search for me and I have found you. I must eat with you today." What a unique gesture that was as the Teacher decided to enter the house of Zacchaeus the sinner with everyone looking. And the criticism specialists began spewing their comments and venom at him. He, that is Christ, perhaps did not know that Zacchaeus was a sinful man, and had he known that he was a sinner, he may not have decided to enter the house of the sinful and outcast Zacchaeus, "for birds of a feather flock together," and so a sinner stays in a sinner's house! But imagine the astonishment, amazement, and joy of Zacchaeus the tax collector, who was probably thinking, "I have always desired and longed to meet him, and here he is going to enter my house and eat with me. He will be my guest, and I will be his host." In fact, we are all God's guests in this life and the hereafter. Oh, what happiness to be accepted by the Lord!

Zacchaeus prepared himself for what he would say to the distinguished guest. So, after Jesus entered his house and sat at the table, Zacchaeus stood up and said to the Teacher in front of everyone, "Thank you, because you were humble enough to enter my house." And he said to the Lord, "Behold, Lord, the half of my goods I will give to the poor. And if I have defrauded anyone of anything, I will restore it fourfold."

This contrition made Zacchaeus great in stature and great in value. His repentance, apostasy, and atonement for his transgressions made the Master, glory be to him, announce publicly in front of everyone: "Today, salvation has come to this house, inasmuch as he too is the son of Abraham." The Son of Man has come to seek those who are lost and save them. He loved much and so was given much, because God wants mercy, not sacrifice. He wants the salvation of sinners, not their destruction.

PRAYING WITH MODESTY AND HUMILITY

Those who pretend to pray in front of everyone so that people will praise them, well, they have received their reward, and there is nothing left for God to do to reward them. They sought their reward from people, not from God, so they received from people what they asked of them. And what they got is worth nothing. God might say to them in the end, "Depart from me, you cursed ones, into the fire prepared for Satan and his angels. I was sick, hungry, thirsty, and imprisoned, but you did not turn to help me."

I remember reading that the Welsh Congregational pastor, Martin Lloyd-Jones (1899–1981) shared that "When I pray, I know and confess that God is my Father, and that He is pleased to bless me. And that He is more willing to give me more than I deserve, and that He always cares about me, and that He always has my best interests at heart and what is best for me. I have to get rid of this feeling, that God stands between me and my desires. I must regard God as my Father, (loving Parent) and He has bought me and paid the price, and this is what is best for me through Jesus Christ. And God waits to bless me with total love through Christ Jesus" (paraphrased).

FASTING IS AN ACT OF HUMILITY

Is fasting an obligation for the Christian? If so, when and how should we fast? The Lord Christ does not give us a specific time for fasting, but he rather tells us, "When you fast, do not be like the hypocrites, for their concern is for people to see them fasting. As for you, you must fast in secret. When you fast, groom yourself and wash your face so that it will not appear to people that you are fasting, but rather turn to your Father, who sees you in secret, and your loving God who sees in secret will reward you" (Matt 6:16–18). A Christian's fasting should not be a burden on society, nor should we impose fasting on others. The late Father Faraj Nakhleh was asked, "Is it necessary for us to fast, and when? If we fast, what should we not eat?" He answered with good intention: "My child, it is good that you fast in order to take care of yourself and not to be on a diet. As for what you eat or what you abstain from eating is not so important because God is not a diet therapist. I say to you: If you fast, God will bless you, and if you do not fast, God will bless you. If you eat and do not fast, so be it. As for what you eat, I say to you: eat as much as you want, eat everything that you want, and eat every day a whole calf. But do not malign your brother or sister. This is the fast. Do not malign one another. The means by which you are measured will be used to measure you, and if there is more added, it will all be taken together."

THE LIFE PROGRAM OF THE CHRISTIAN

THE LORD'S FASTING IF YOU WERE THE SON OF GOD

The fasting of the Lord Jesus, glory be to God, was in keeping with the traditions, conventions, and customs of his people. It was more about the need to abstain from earthly goods in order to devote himself to eternal goods. So he fasted in order to commune with God in heaven, and his fasting was not only to fulfil the law but in response to the love of God. He fasted in order to soliloquize with God in heaven and to remember and remind us that we need every word that comes from the mouth of God. His acute hunger intensified to commune with the loving God.

His great fast, or the forty days of Lent, was a preparation for the great work: the work of redemption. His fasting was a reclusion with his loving God and preparation for the redemption of humans from sin. It is the restoration of life after forty years in the desert with God's company and under God's care.

He fasted for forty days. The number forty symbolizes the forty years of wandering in the Sinai desert after leaving the slavery of Egypt. Jesus would often seclude himself in order to sit in the presence of his heavenly Father.[4] And during this fast, when he was about to go out into the world after fasting for forty days, then the Adversary, Satan, came to tempt him. It is as if Jesus began facing many choices in order to begin his public work of salvation, and he may have been hungry. I think that his hunger was physical, and it was also and especially a spiritual hunger. He longed to go out in front of the crowds of people, and perhaps he wondered what he would say to them. What should he teach them? He was challenged in several ways (Matt 4:1–11)!

1. Then the Adversary approached the Giver of Life, suggesting that he turn the stones into bread so he could eat, he the one who gives every good blessing and every perfect gift to those who are hungry and thirsty for righteousness and gives his disciples something to eat. "If you are the Son of God, order

---

4. Again, we are using the term for God as Father, perhaps more in keeping with what Jesus said.

The Sermon on the Mount

these stones to become bread, so you and those with you will eat." The Teacher looked at him and said, "Man does not live by bread alone." He silenced Satan, and he refused to submit to magic or to Satan.

2. Next, the Adversary took him to Jerusalem, to the Temple of Solomon, and offered him another opportunity: "If you are the Son of God, throw yourself down," a depth of more than fifty meters, and the people would see that he jumped, and they would rush to see what happened to this poor soul. Would there be anything left of him? Upon approaching, they would see that he was safe and sound, as if he had not fallen from the top to the bottom. In other words, the Adversary offered to use a dishonest trick so that people would believe in him, but he refused, saying, "Do not put the Lord your God to the test." He did not surrender to evil because he wanted to teach that we humans have free will. We are not those robbed of our will and the ability to make hard decisions.

3. Then the Adversary took him back to the top of the mountain, showed him all the kingdoms in the vicinity of Jericho, and said to him, "All this I will give to you if you bow your head and worship me," because he, the Adversary, claimed he had been given authority over these kingdoms. The Lord, glory be to him, did not consent but rather rebuked Satan, saying to him, "Begone, Satan! For it is written, 'You must kneel to the Lord your God, and worship only Him.'"

Then, after these trials to prepare for his public life, there was only one way left for him where Satan could not resist and so challenged him. It was Jesus fully in the presence of the loving God. "There is no greater love than that of one who gives his or her life for friends." Then angels appeared to serve him.

The Life Program of the Christian

TO GATHER IN UNITY WITH THE CHILDREN OF GOD

What remained for Jesus the Christ to redeem those who were under the law? How would he gather the dispersed children of God? How might he demolish the wall separating the children of God so there would no longer be Jew or gentile, neither man nor woman, nor master nor slave? How could he empower humanity to become, once again, one family, whose Lord is God and whose savior is Jesus Christ? We learn that one goal of Christ's redemption was to gather in unity God's scattered children.

There is only one means left before Christ the Savior, none greater, more refined, or nobler than this: "There is no greater love than that of a man who gives his life for his friends."[5] This is what the Lord did when he took the form of a slave and became obedient to the point of death, even death on the cross. He is the one who assured us, "When I am lifted up from the earth, I will draw everyone to me; I rise from the earth to the cross, I rise from the cross to the grave, I rise from the grave to heaven" (John 12:32). This is the fasting of the Lord, glory be to God. This is our destiny if we take up our cross and follow Christ. The cross made the Jews doubt Christ, and the Greeks considered it a sign of the Christians' ignorance, but for us, it is God's wisdom (Matt 28:1–10).

OUR LENT

Our fasting for forty days (Lent) is nothing but a renewal of Christ's fasting and the identification with the greatest "faster," Jesus Christ. The number forty became a number laden with meanings: forty years of wandering in the desert, preparing to enter the Holy Land, the promised land, and forty days of the fasting of Christ the Lord in preparation for his entry into the kingdom of his heavenly Father. This led to his charge: "Repent, for the kingdom of heaven is at hand" (Matt 3:2). The forty days from resurrection to ascension

---

5. Again, given the nature of this quote, there is reference to a man representing humankind.

was a period of preparation for a life-changing event, important and vital work, and the beginning of announcing the good news that the reign of God was near. The forty days is a sacred number for Christians and Jews because we fast together. This is the case so that we may unite with the Savior, not so that people may praise us. We fast in order to pass from slavery to freedom. Therefore, you, when you fast, groom yourself and wash your face so that it will not appear to people that you are fasting, but rather so your God will see you in secret, and your God who sees in secret will reward you (Matt 6:16).[6] This is the true way to fast, not a physical exercise to lose weight. Christ's fasting is not an act performed for the masses; it is in the desert where he is alone with his loving God. So, if you give to charity, do it secretly, and let your left hand not know what your right hand has done. The fasting of the Christian should be a call to all people to renounce their sins and glorify God. "O Lord of Hosts, be with us, for in times of distress, we have no helper but you. O Lord of Hosts, have mercy on us."

Fasting is linked to charity. "Be careful not to perform your charity in front of people in order for them to see you and glorify you." When you give charity, your left hand should not know what your right hand has done, and your God, who sees in secret, will reward you. Charity to the poor is like charity to God. You share with the poor the good things that God has shared with you. Everything I gave during my life, I found on the day I died, and everything I was attached to during my life, I lost on the day I died.

Charity is given as if it were charity to Christ Jesus himself. Charity comes from God's money with which you have been entrusted so that you may be perfect, just as your God is perfect. Whatever you gave to any one of these, my little brothers and sisters, you gave to me. And you will receive your reward publicly from God who sees in secret. Charity is one of the basic components of a person's relationship with God. So, how can we build a relationship with God whom we do not see when there is no relationship between us and our brother and sister whom we see?

---

6. Another place where it may be wise to leave the masculine "Father" as a reference to God.

How can we expect charity from God if we harden our hearts before our oppressed fellow human beings?

"Hallowed be your name!" This prayer means giving special and distinct respect to God. In the ancient Jewish tradition, it was forbidden to pronounce the name of the Divine glory, and they replaced it with the title "The Name." It is strange that obscene, vulgar words have entered our colloquial language. We use swear words and insults in the name of God, and our children often dare to blaspheme God in their ordinary conversations. For the first time, I heard vulgar, dirty, and obscene blasphemy, may God forgive them, from young men chatting in the early hours of the night near the Ontosh (parish house) where I lived. They were suggesting that God got married, a blasphemous statement intended to shame his wife. I ask your forgiveness, O God, I ask your forgiveness! O Lord, set a guard over their mouths and a watchman at the door of their lips. If you kept a record of sins, O Lord, who will persist? You have the fountain of forgiveness, and by your light, we will see the light. May your mercy be upon us according to our trust in you. God will hold us accountable for every superfluous word that will come out of our mouths, because that which is more than "Yes, Yes" or "No, No" often comes from the Evil One.

PRAYER OF THE NAIVE PEASANT IN THE CHURCH OF ARS

"Thy kingdom come; thy will be done, on earth as it is in heaven." The will of God is not attained through many words but rather through the presence before God and the Spirit of God in our lives. This reminds me of Father Vianney, the priest of Ars in France, which was a poor village where people lived by farming their land. There was a poor and illiterate old man who used to come to church every morning at five o'clock and stay until six o'clock. Then he would get up and go to his field all day. His daily presence attracted the attention of the parish priest, Father Vianney. He found it strange that this old man would come to church every day in summer and winter, sit for an hour looking at the Holy Eucharist, and then go, returning the next day. The priest of Ars was astonished at what this simple peasant was doing who came to church with mud covering his shoes, whose hands were very rough from his work in the field. So he approached him one day and asked him, "My son, I see you coming very early to church every morning, staying there for an hour, and then disappearing. What do you do in church?" The elderly man replied, "Father, I come to church, pray my daily prayer, and go to work on my land." The priest said to him, "You pray?! What do you say for an hour every day?" The poor old man replied, "Father, I do not know how to pray, because I did not go to school. I come to church, I look at him and he looks at me, then I get up and go to work in my field."

The reign of God on earth is trust in the hands of the believers in Christ and in the hands of those searching for the meaning of life. The will of God is that every human being will be saved, that sin be destroyed, and that sinners are saved. God does not want the death of sinners but rather their return to divine providence and love. Our God is not a god of war, violence, and disasters but of mercy, love, truth, and reconciliation. The kingdom of God is for God to reign in the hearts of people, and God makes the final decision, and the decision is to love and save the sinner and not destroy any of them.

All of God's creation is good, whether human, animal, or plant. Look at the birds in the sky. They do not plant or store in granaries, and our loving God provides for them. God is not called simply "their Father" but rather "your heavenly Father" who provides for them because of his generosity and love that does what is good. The apostle Paul tells us in his letters, "Rejoice in union with the Lord always! I will say it again: rejoice! Let your love for all people be seen. The Lord is near! Do not worry about anything, but in every case, make your needs known to God by prayer and supplication along with thanksgiving. Then the peace of God that surpasses all understanding keeps your hearts and your minds in Christ Jesus" (Phil 4:4–7).

The Life Program of the Christian

BLESSED ARE THOSE WHO HUNGER AND THIRST FOR RIGHTEOUSNESS, FOR THEY WILL BE FILLED

Jesus Christ is the one who thirsts and hungers the most for righteousness, and we follow him. Whoever follows him does not walk in darkness (John 12:46). Woe to those who close their eyes and deafen their ears so as not to see or hear the hungry and the thirsty, but double woe to anyone who starves people and deprives them of water, for they will perish in eternal hunger and thirst. Lebanon is a country of people who are hungry for a good life, a country where active water springs abound, yet it is a thirsty country. It is a country with many resources, yet a hungry people. The ones who starve the people are natives of the country. They are the rulers responsible for providing bread and water for their people. Yet they act like wolves. Instead of bread, they offer stones, and instead of water, they offer colocynth.

They will leave this life and everything they have accumulated, and when they come before the Creator, they will be asked, "What have you done to these little children of mine? You heard them say, 'I was hungry, but you gave me no food; thirsty, but you gave me nothing to drink; a stranger, but you did not give me shelter; naked, needing clothes, but you did not give them to me; sick, but you did not visit me.'" Then they will wonder why God did not step in and help them. They may ask why these hungry and thirsty strangers, people needing clothes, and sick people were not taken care of "by you, O Almighty God?" God will answer them calmly and with deep sadness: "Whatever you did not do to one of the least of these, my brothers and sisters, you did not do to me. You attained your happiness in your life, and yet the poor suffered. Your service to them would be my service to them."

With my tearful sadness for thousands of young people, children, mothers, and the elderly, I pity the blind-hearted, heedless holders of power who enumerate their possessions, count their money, and rob the poor, not caring about the day of judgment, not caring about the Master approaching them and saying to them,

"Today your soul will be taken from you, so the things you have gathered, whose will they be?" They will have no answer because the blind do not see, and the mute do not speak. And the rulers of this world are the same, unwilling to respond. They have ears but do not hear, they have eyes but do not see, and hearts that do not have mercy. They neglect their responsibility. Their first and last concern is to accumulate money. They hoard money in the bank and fence the property with barbed wire. Thus, they lay up for themselves treasures on earth, where the worm feeds, the moth destroys, and the thief steals.

Their money is the bread of the poor, and their barriers prevent water from getting to the thirsty. They will leave behind everything they have collected when they appear before the Creator with their deeds, whether good or bad. They will understand that God is not partial to any person. They spent their lives eating and enjoying themselves, filling their bellies with food and collecting the good things of this world while their brothers and sisters were standing in the streets and on the roads shouting, "Help us, for our stomachs are empty, our lips are dry, and we want a drop of water. You are ignorant and deprive us of what God has bestowed upon all of us. You have taken away everything, not caring that one day the Lord will come near, and with fire he will judge all people. We are famished, and we pray for your retreat to God, and for you to help your suffering people." The poor are the ones who will judge you before God, and those who surrounded the manger are the ones who will sit on the thrones on the day of judgment to judge you. These people are why Jesus came with love, and why we, as those who follow Jesus, must help those who are hungry and thirsty.

CHAPTER THREE

The Companions and Conversations of Jesus

"The twelve were with him, as well as some of the women who had been cured of evil spirits and infirmities: Mary, called Magdalene, from whom seven demons had gone out, and Joanna, the wife of Herod's steward Chu'za and Susanna, and many others, who provided for them out of their resources."

(LUKE 8:1B–3)

IN MY REFLECTIONS, I have often looked for the people who had a role in the life of the Teacher, and I have discovered many. Among them were a few special women, including Mary, Jesus's mother, and they had central role in the life of the Lord, glory be to him. I have learned so much from the dedication of these women about following the teachings of the Sermon on the Mount. One night, while I was asleep, the telephone rang, awakening me. I got up to answer the phone, very excited to write about what I had experienced the night before: the profound insight that many women are wonderful models of those who follow Jesus with deep dedication and loyalty. It was a "wake-up" call for me, a special moment when I saw the importance of women in the life of Jesus clearly!

In addition, when the phone rang, I became immediately aware that the Christian's pathway could easily be summarized in the Sermon on the Mount. I suddenly saw that everything about my Christian faith went back to the Sermon on the Mount. A phone call in the middle of the night woke me up to reality that all of the Teacher's teachings were within the framework of what he announced in the Sermon on the Mount and that I had seen it right in front of me in the women who were in my life.

I do not know if I can express, in simple words, what I wholeheartedly lived and experienced that entire night. It was a unique blessing. I understood that I must continue on the path of following the teachings of the Sermon on the Mount and have this teaching give me insight on how to live and how to teach others about the spiritual life. We are to contribute in our special way to the establishment of God's reign, and the many women in the life of Jesus were a model of how we are to serve. We are transformed to advance the reign of God, and may his name be honored and may his kingdom come.[1]

CHRIST FULFILLS THE LAW AND THE PROPHECIES

"I did not come to call the righteous, but the sinners" (Luke 5:32), because the loving God rejoices more when one sinner repents than other persons who consider themselves good and yet do not feel the need to repent. God is joyful when the sinner receives the embrace of God. In our time especially, there seem to be many people who do not turn to God, perhaps because they have houses that are warm and their money is abundant. They don't sense the need to turn to God, but their hearts may be empty; they too need God's embrace.

God reaches out to everyone, receives in love the magi and shepherds who are poor gentiles (*goyim*), and extends love and healing power to the lepers, epileptics, the disabled, the blind, and

---

1. In this case, the word "kingdom," given its use across time, is perhaps the best way for me to describe what I felt.

the deaf. It is also interesting that the references of this healing power are usually about men, as if the society is made up of only men, and the women are marginalized in nearly all areas of life. Even when he multiplied the loaves of bread, only the men were counted: "Those who ate were about five thousand men, besides women and children" (Matt 14:21). This reference suggests that there were different roles for men and women, and that the men tended to be those in power. Yet Jesus invited all people, women and men, to receive the Lord, glory be to God, during his preaching about the forthcoming reign of God. He did not discriminate against women. They became members of Christ's family, and Jesus said, "Come to me, you who are weary, and I will give you rest" (Matt 11:28). Jesus invites everyone to receive God's love, taking into account the structures of society. No one is left out; he is sensitive to the circumstances of all who come his way.

For example, Jesus met Nicodemus, who came to him at night for fear of the Jews as Jesus had become an outcast, having threatened their authority in the temple. Jesus met Simeon, who was a righteous and venerable old man. He was the one who announced while carrying the baby Jesus in his arms, "Now you release your servant, O Lord, in peace according to your word, for my eyes have seen your salvation, which you have prepared in the sight of all peoples, a light for all nations and the glory of your people Israel" (Luke 2:29-32). After that, he met the rich young man who wanted to supplement his wealth and improve his life by getting closer to God (Matt 19:16-22). He asked the Teacher, "What should I do to inherit eternal life?" The Teacher said to him, "Go and do as the Samaritan did," after having given him the parable of the good Samaritan. That is, be a merciful Samaritan, and do not be an arrogant priest or Levite who does not care about the poor or the needy. Do not honor Jesus with your lips while your heart is far from him; do good, do justice to the orphan, and be just with the widows. Jesus did not leave anyone out and honored the context of their life.

The rich young man wanted to follow Christ and said he would follow him anywhere in order to inherit eternal life. The

Teacher answered him, "Go and sell everything you have, distribute it to the poor, and come, follow me" (Matt 19–21). The rich young man withdrew because he had a lot of money. The Teacher was sad for him and said to the disciples, "It is easier for a camel to pass through the eye of a needle than for a rich man to enter the kingdom of heaven" (Mark 10:25). It is difficult for a person who is rich and attached to worldly possessions to receive and embrace the reign of God. This fact does not mean that every rich person is cursed or destined for hell. Rather, every rich person who places all his hope and faith in the money that is desired by the poor person, or every poor person who places all his hope and faith in the money available to the rich person, will both not likely find their way to heaven. This means that every person who hoards up treasures on earth will find it difficult to honor and worship two masters: God and money. The one who does will either hate this and love that or scorn that and be loyal to this. This is a reminder to us that birds have nests and animals in the wild have dens, but the Son of God has no place (stone) on which to lay his head. The Master was sad for the rich man because he preferred money more than following the Teacher, that is, to embrace the reign of God. In our country, there are many stones and many people, but those who follow Jesus may have no stone on which to lay their head.

THE SAMARITAN WOMAN, FIRST HERALD OF CHRIST

Jesus also met the Samaritan woman, and her story is exciting in many ways. She, a woman, became the first herald of the coming of Christ. There were lepers and blind people crying out, "Jesus, Son of David, have mercy on us." The Teacher would summon them and approach them, asking, "What would you want me to do for you?" Some would answer, "I want to see," the other, "I want to hear," another, "If you want, cleanse me of my illness." There was a paralyzed man with no one to help him to go down to the pool of Siloam to be healed. Jesus went to him and asked: "Do you want to be healed?" The paralyzed man answered out of despair, "Of course, I want to be cured, but I have no hope that anyone will help me get into the water, the first step." When a person despairs of getting people's help, they often turn to God, and the Son of Mary says to him, "Get up, pick up your bed, and walk." And the man stood upright. There was blind person whom Jesus met who was blind from birth; it provided an occasion for the Teacher to teach us that neither that person nor his parents had sinned which caused him to be born blind. But the glory of God was revealed in him as his sight returned. How were we so privileged to get this Redeemer? He has the answer for everyone who believes in him, regardless of their circumstances. There was light in his life, and he gave hope to all people and invited them to find the path we all have to follow.

He also met Lazarus and his friends, and he met the son of the widow of Nain, whom he brought back to life and handed over to his mother, turning her tears of sadness into tears of joy at the return of her son. Months later, another widowed mother would lose her son on the cross and would only be consoled by seeing him rise from the dead.

He met those who crucified him, those who flogged him, mocked him, and spat in his face, and he raised his voice to the loving God, saying and beseeching: "O Father, forgive them, for they do not know what they do" (Luke 23:32–34). There are no hateful, nor vengeful, nor mocking people worse than these, and for their sake, he begged God, saying, "Father, forgive them, for they do not know what they do." He did not expect an apology or repentance from them, but rather, he uttered those words and took his last breath. The Master, to whom be glory, was not restricted by what people did for him. He listened to the voice of God and acted according to God's message: he came so that we may have life, life in its fullest measure. He came to redeem those who hated him and called them to repentance. "He who wants to follow me, let them carry the cross and follow me; I will give them rest for I am gentle and humble at heart" (Matt 10:38).

The Sermon on the Mount

WHO IS YOUR BROTHER? THE MERCIFUL SAMARITAN

You Be a Merciful Samaritan

He (the Samaritan) ran into the Jew lying between life and death on the side of the road; he came face to face with the one who represented lost and shattered humanity. Feeling compassion for the Jew, he bowed his head, washed the Jew's wounds, carried him on his animal, and took him back to the hotel where he cared for him. When the rich young man came to test him, asking, "Who is my brother?," Jesus answered, "Go and do as you have heard; be a good Samaritan, and do not be an evil Levite or indifferent to the sick or those in need of help." In other words, be a good Muslim or a merciful Jew, and do not be an evil or unjust Christian who is indifferent to sick humanity or to those close to you who are destitute and do not know God. In reality, this merciful Samaritan symbolizes Jesus himself, and the Jew is the symbol of the chosen people and of wounded humanity. Who will pity her and stain her hands to heal her? Christ used the Samaritan man, the Samaritan woman, and all Samaritans who are in real life socially outcast and ostracized traditionally as examples of the children of God who are scattered but through their good deeds are closer to God. They are eager to meet the awaited messiah. His brothers and sisters are every human being who were born as children in the image and likeness of God.

JESUS CHOOSES HIS DISCIPLES

Jesus chose his first disciples exclusively from men, most of whom were fishermen from around the Sea of Galilee. It would have been easy for them to travel together. All of them were men from Galilee, except for Iscariot (Qaryouti), who was from the town of Qaryout near Jerusalem. What brought him to the place around the lake? Did this stranger come to Galilee to deliver the Lord into sinful hands?! Iscariot became the embodiment of betrayal, as we read: "Judas, are you betraying the Son of Man with a kiss?" (Luke 22:48).

He chose only men not out of contempt for women but out of consideration for all women, who should be respected. It was in keeping with the conditions prevailing in his society at the time that unmarried women would not travel with men without some conditions that gave them privacy. He did not want to lose his credibility and be accused of not respecting or observing the law. In Judaism, a woman was occasionally considered a "thing," an object, not a person. In Islam, she is often just a pronoun, but in Christianity, she is a human person, made in the image and likeness of God, equal to man in all rights and privileges. Humans were created in the image and likeness of God: man and woman he created them, in his image and likeness he created them (Gen 1:27). Humanity, therefore, needed Jesus Christ to restore the woman's dignity and status.

WOMEN AMONG THE DISCIPLES

Jesus had honorable and generous women serving him, and he respected and cared for them. We read, for example, about one of the women who came to him for help. We read that "her sins have been forgiven, because she loved much" (Luke 7:47). In the life of Jesus, there was first his immaculate virgin mother and then the many women named Mary or Miriam who followed him to Jerusalem. These women cared for him and wept over him. He said to them: "Do not weep for me, but weep for your children. O Jerusalem, O Jerusalem, you kill the prophets and stone those who are sent to you. How many times have I wanted to gather your children together, as a hen gathers her chicks under her wings, but you refused? Behold, your house is left unto you desolate" (Matt 23:37–39).

Likewise, there were Mary and Martha, the sisters of Lazarus, the one who died and was raised by Jesus from the dead. Also, there was Mary Magdalene who washed Jesus's feet with perfume and about whom the Lord, glory be to him, said that she was forgiven much because she loved much. And there was the Samaritan woman who asked, "Is he the awaited Messiah?" She said to her family and to the people of her village, "Come and see a man who told me everything I did. Is he the Awaited Messiah?" Thus, she became the first herald of Christ. He did not view women as an inferior element, and he was obedient to one woman, the virgin Mary, throughout his life on earth. Did he not say to his mother at the wedding in Cana of Galilee, "Woman, my time has not yet come," yet he complied with her command, and performed his first miracle among the people? Afterward she said to the servants, "Do whatever he tells you." Can we forget that the first person to witness the Lord's resurrection was a woman, Mary Magdalene, and she quickly went to announce to the disciples that the Lord was not in the grave? She said, "His grave is empty, the stone has been rolled away, and the light shines from the grave. He has truly risen. He has risen. He appeared to me, and I thought he was the gardener. Come and see that the tomb is empty. The messenger commanded me to tell you that he is going to Galilee ahead of you, and there you will see Him" (John 19:41).

Jesus respected every human being because he believed that every human being was born a child in the image and likeness of

God. He believed that God created man and woman in the divine image and likeness. Jesus did not come to abolish the law but to fulfill it, to restore human dignity, for man and woman together are the image and likeness of God.

How beautiful it is in the company of the Lord and walking with him! How good and how wonderful it is to revive what he did during his life on earth and on our land, especially in Galilee, our Galilee, the Galilee of the nations, so that the people walking in the darkness are able to see; a great light has dawned on them. The angels complete the good news to the shepherds: "Do not be afraid, for I bring you good news of great joy, for to us, a child has been born, and a son has been given."

THE LORD'S PRAYER

In the Lord's Prayer (Matt 6:9–15), Jesus Christ teaches us to ask for three "gifts" from God: Our Father, who art in heaven,

- give us this day our daily bread;
- forgive us our trespasses, as we forgive those who trespass against us; and
- lead us not into temptation, but deliver us from evil... Amen.

These three pleas sum up everything a believer needs. Through these three requests, the Teacher gathered all the needs of the believer: our physical needs, our mental needs, and our spiritual needs. These three pleas contain what we need: bread for the body, forgiveness for one's kin, and guidance to follow the will of God. Jesus teaches that humans are created in the image and likeness of God and that he gave them the capacity to be in relationship with God and each other. Yet they may still be tempted, so the prayer says, "Lead us not into temptation, but deliver us from evil." No matter how diverse our needs are, they are covered in these requests. This is the genius of Jesus Christ. How could it not be, since he is the Creator? "All things came into being through him, and without him not one thing came into being" (John 1:3). He taught us to say, "Our Father who art in heaven, hallowed be thy name; thy kingdom come; thy will be done on Earth as it is in heaven."

Immediately after seeking the glory of God in all the ports of life and in heaven, Christ the Lord moves on to the importance of the body and the importance of its needs so that we may live, remain alive, and continue our lives. After that, the Divine Teacher moves us in the prayer to the purity of the body and the rejection of sin. And finally, the prayer is a request to remain far from evil, from sin and its forces. In a comprehensive sense, Jesus Christ teaches us that we are alive and need to remain alive. That is why I must be aware of my unworthiness: "Against you alone I have sinned, and done evil in your sight," and from you alone I seek help. My life needs to constantly revert to God, the Almighty, because purifying my being from temptation is what makes me enter into companionship and communion with God. True life is communion with God through Jesus Christ, so I need the forgiveness of sins in order to live in the company of God and under God's protection. We might summarize this part of the prayer in one sentence: "Enjoy life with God, and enjoy the fullness of life thanks to our Lord and Savior Jesus Christ."

The request, "Give us this day our daily bread," is much broader than asking for the subsistence bread provides. It is a comprehensive sentence for all our daily needs. Our daily bread means that we believe that our life in all its details is a blessing from God and dependent on God the Creator. We include in this request our acknowledgment of God's grace and his all-encompassing power. We ask God, the Almighty, that the sun continues to shine, the moon continues to appear, and that in winter, it will rain. The earth will yield what we need. It is within God's power to stop the rain, darken the sun, and make the land barren and unyielding. He also assured us, through the words of Jesus Christ, that our hairs are counted and not a single hair will fall out without the will of the God of love. When we beseech God to give us our daily bread (which means we ask for all that will make our entire lives one of health and purpose), we will not lack any of the necessities for life. It does not include asking for extras and luxuries—only our daily bread. Our daily bread includes our need for peace, for reassurance, for love, for forgiveness, and for tolerance. It also includes a calm world and beautiful weather and to keep earthquakes, fire, and floods away from us. We pray that we respect nature and enjoy its beauty, because it is a gift from God that we often ignore. Our daily bread is an ecumenical prayer and the Creator's orientation toward creation.

This request includes all aspects of life. We ask God because God is the loving Parent who gives us good gifts. This is a broad and comprehensive request. It is an acknowledgment of God's power and grace upon us and God's generosity in giving us every blessing and every good so that our lives may be as close to God as possible, taking into account that we are sinners. For this reason exclusively, the Son of God was incarnated to rise from the cross: to lift us up, forgive our sins and shortcomings, and bury them with him in the grave. He buries all our sins in the grave in death, and he returns and brings us back to life, to resurrection purity. It means that "you who were baptized into Christ, have worn Christ"(Rom 6:3).

THE NEW PERSON IN THE IMAGE OF GOD

Paul tells us, "Put off the old person, and put on the new person, which was renewed in baptism with spirit and fire" (Matt 9:17). The new person means living the Sermon on the Mount according to the teachings of the Lord, the original lawgiver. We live the law free from the legalism of the scribes and Pharisees so that God may be glorified in our actions. We use the Sabbath to serve others, and we respect the entire law. Sin begins from the heart, from the eyes, from the possessions, and from adultery, from worshiping money and only caring for material goods.

Nevertheless, we ask God to forgive us our sins. This does not mean that we have been made virtuous by Jesus Christ as much as it means that salvation through Jesus Christ requires the confession of sins. We are all sinners, and no one is perfect but God alone. We can say "forgive us our sins" after we have acknowledged that God is our loving Father and by praying, "Our Father, who art in heaven." We turn to God as children of God. We are confident that when we make a mistake, slip up, or neglect our duty towards God and towards our neighbor, we are still loved by God. If we neglect to take care of one another, and humans have been prone to sin since birth, then we will need to return to God in repentance, aware that God is love. God forgives us if we confess our transgressions and sins. In short, this request is the prayer of children to their loving Parent with a feeling of belonging and true love, the same feeling as that of the prodigal son who said, "Father, I am not worthy to be called your son, so make me as one of your hired workers" (Luke 7:6). It is enough for me to look at Jesus Christ and the many torments he endured for me so that I, in turn, can forgive everyone who has tried to insult me or sinned against me. So I pray, "Forgive us our trespasses, as we forgive those who trespass against us. Our Father-mother in heaven, I am a sinner, and I am in need of your love and your forgiveness. I am an imperfect human being, and I hope that God will forgive me, just as I forgive my fellow human beings. May you, dear God, complement my weakness with your unconditional love for humanity." We need to forgive those who transgress against us, that is, to imitate Christ who forgave us all our sins and continues to forgive all our sins. He is the one who prayed on the cross, saying, "Father, forgive them, for they do not know what they do." He has forgiven us seventy times seven times every day. His forgiveness while on the cross is still the greatest and most eloquent proof of the divinity of Christ. Only God can forgive the sins of those who crucified Jesus, forgive his enemies, pardoned those who curse him. Jesus asks God for their forgiveness in that they did not know what they had done.

We continue our supplications to our loving Parent in heaven, saying, "Lead us not into temptation, but deliver us from evil." This is completed by Jesus's declaration to his disciples: "Stay awake, and pray that you will not be put to temptation." The supplication "deliver us from evil" is a broader request than just delivering us from the devil who tempts us. It is rather to ask, "Deliver us from every situation or every form of temptation to sin." "Deliver us from evil" means deliver us from ourselves: from greed, vanity, and selfishness. Deliver us from every other form of evil that lurks in our hearts. Save us from Satan and all his traps. We make this universal plea, "Deliver us from evil," so that our relationship with God remains undiminished.

We must pay attention to the fact that there is a conclusion to this Lord's Prayer: "For yours is the kingdom, the power, and the glory forever." This is a confession of faith that God has the ability to provide what we have previously asked. We end our prayer as we have begun it: by giving glory to God. Out of the burning love for God in our hearts, we end our prayers by giving glory to God and by surrendering our minds, souls, and lives as a ratification of all of the above and with our acknowledgment that God has the kingdom, power, and glory forever and ever, amen. This is a declaration of faith in God's power.

HEAVENLY TREASURE

We move forward in the Sermon on the Mount, trying to understand what it means and to grasp the meaning that our treasure is both in heaven and on earth. We must constantly remember that we are children of our loving God in heaven, and that, as the prophet Elijah said, "I am standing before God," and that the eye of God looks after us. Therefore, whatever I do, the first priority I give is not to what people say about me or even what I say about myself. You do not need to evaluate yourself; leave the evaluation to God. If you give charity, it should not be for a feeling of self-worthiness, nor for what people say about you, but let your charity be for the sake of helping the poor and sharing in God's bounties. Likewise, I should not pray so that people will say about me, "What a great man of prayer!" My prayer must be before God and the divine presence. We must give the world its due and God his due, because what is Caesar's belongs to Caesar, and what is God's belongs to God. We do not pray so that the world can see us and praise us. That is why Jesus told us, "When you pray, go into your room," meaning, be alone and close your door. In other words, stop caring what people say about you. "Pray to your Father who sees in secret, and your Father who sees will reward you openly" (Matt 6:5–6).

The Lord tells us what to do "when [we] pray." God does not tell us where to pray or how many times to pray—only how to pray "when [you] pray," whether it is one time or several times. Whenever you pray, remember that you are communicating with the Creator, acknowledging God's parenthood and acknowledging God's generosity. For God makes the sun rise on the evil and on the righteous and sends rain down on everyone without distinction. Do not care about the world, that is, do not exaggerate and focus your attention on the world or the needs of the body, but focus your being before God and leave the world and its temptations. Carry your cross and follow God who is the light, the truth, and the life. Following Christ means that we follow the path that Christ charts for us, not that we chart a path and expect Christ to follow us.

Secluding ourselves in prayer represents our focus on our relationships with God, who gives us every good gift and every perfect talent (Matt 25:14–30). It is not easy for a person to be a Christian. It is not easy to be born from above. The Master, glory be to him, while he was still among us in the flesh, was subject to temptation from Satan. Thus, a true Christian faces the world and its temptations as Jesus did. We have no help or refuge other than resorting to God in seclusion and in supplication to the Creator, the Almighty, in contrition and in following the law of God. Therefore, the Christian resorts to some mortal acts such as giving, fasting, and charity. The path that we must take is the Sermon on the Mount. It is a summary of the central message of the Holy Bible. We need not create a path for ourselves in life; rather, we should follow the path that God has drawn for us.

Jesus Christ continues his teaching to those who took the Beatitudes as their credentials to preach the good news, warning his disciples not to lay up for themselves treasures on earth, where thieves steal and the moth devours. Rather, he urges them to lay up for themselves treasures in heaven, where the moth does not consume and the thief does not steal. The Master, to whom be glory, puts before us two choices: either we can be with him and not store up treasures for ourselves on earth, or we could not be with him and store up treasures for ourselves on earth. If we choose him, then we will have our treasures in heaven, where there is neither a thief nor a tempter but guaranteed eternal security by God himself (Matt 6:5–6).

In the first part of this prayer (which is negative), "Do not lay up for yourselves treasures on Earth," Jesus Christ does not only mean financial treasures but something broader. "Treasures" is a term much broader than just money. Rather, it is an attachment to the possessions of this world and the desire to have the goods of this world. This leads to the love of power, domination of others, and the love of our prestige before people. Instead, we should be humble and leave behind these empty quests of this world. Every exaggerated attachment to the goods of this world represents treasures on earth, such as luxurious clothes that cost thousands of dollars which some wealthy people may wear in order to show off their material wealth in front of people and to appear in people's eyes more beautiful and handsome than the Almighty God created them to be. They hide their true selves in an effort to beautify God's creation, but, in reality, there is nothing more beautiful than what God created. Possessions are what often hide the spiritual poverty of the rich. Treasures on earth are often the passion of the poor who exaggerate the benefit in collecting money; it does not lead to happiness, nor does the passion of people who want all the luxuries of life. They spend thousands of dollars on clothes that they wear once, along with shoes and accessories. This is the way they try to show people that they are beautiful and powerful. In reality, it is the human being who is beautiful, created in the image of God. The most beautiful thing about it is God's creation of beauty and purity. Even priests show off in their transient clothes or their fancy cars or even in their advanced degrees in order to show people how rich, powerful, and educated they are. These actions become like a light that does not reveal the way but rather a light that blinds the eyes and fosters doubt in the hearts of the weak.

It is somewhat easy to store up treasures for ourselves on earth, but it is very difficult for us to store up treasures in heaven, including humility, mercy, and the love for God. Limiting happiness to obtaining a social or religious rank or the success of a family member are in themselves treasures on earth.

THE CLOTHES OF HAPPINESS

Let us remember the prince who wanted to wear the clothes of happiness. He traveled to all corners of the earth looking for a happy person to buy those clothes, but he did not find anyone. However, in the end, he found a poor farmer plowing his land, singing and repeating, "By God, I will not humiliate you, my soul." The prince asked him, "Are you happy?" He replied, "I am happy, sir." So, the prince asked to buy his clothes, and the farmer replied, "Sir, I do not have a shirt. The shirt of happiness cannot be bought. It is a gift from God to those who fear him. Being satisfied with a little and being content to live by sharing with deprived persons constitute the surest treasure in heaven."

TWO STORIES FROM LIFE

It so happened that a person wanted to baptize his son, so he borrowed money to rent ten buses to Haifa. The priest asked him to save the money that he would pay for the ten buses, and he (that is, the priest) would give him the same amount to buy clothes for his wife and children. But he became angry with the priest. Still, the priest accompanied him from his village to Mount Carmel in his own car voluntarily, even though he did not have the money for gasoline for the car. The priest chose the kind way to help.

Likewise, another man who lived in a semi-hut had a baby boy, so he brought him home from the hospital by helicopter and named him after the Israeli minister of defense at the time. He said, "Look, people, I am bringing my wife and young son back by plane to the village!" But his happiness was the return of his wife and son, not impressing people with the use of the helicopter.

The treasures in heaven are not material treasures; neither money, authority, power, nor oppression of the weak can constitute treasures in heaven. Mariam Bewardi said, "In heaven, we find all vices forgiven, and we do not find pride. In hell, we find all virtues condemned, and we do not find humility."[2] It is useful to mention the clever but unjust servant who, before his master cast him out, began to reduce the debts of the debtors to his master, so that when he got expelled, they would receive him in their homes. It was the wrong motivation. But heaven's treasures are receiving with mercy and sacrificing earthly goods. True happiness is loving God and loving the people in your life. Everything that a person treasures or uses is to help others. "All that you did to one of these poor brothers of mine, you did to me" (Matt 25:40). We thus record a treasure for ourselves in heaven. "If you give a cup of cold water to a thirsty person in my name, you will receive a hundredfold in heaven" (Matt 10:42). These treasures are not only the help we provide to those in need, but they are also a return to God through our words and actions, including our material giving. I remember, with thanks, the lady whom I had not met from the countries in the west who wrote to me, "I read your book, and I identified with you in your work, and for that reason, I am sending you all my savings from the past month." Inside the envelope was a bank check for ten dollars. It was a heartfelt gift. We recognize that "every good gift and every perfect talent" is from God's generosity. God places them in our hands. It is by renunciation of pride, selfishness, material greed, and longing for earthly goods that we give up. It is in humility and gratitude before the Great Giver, the Source of virtues and giving, that we give our true treasures. In fact, it is in giving up the vices of pride, selfishness, material and spiritual greed, and contempt that we find our way, not so much as a concession but rather a renunciation. It is throwing these things away and rising above them all that is important. We do not give up sin, but we rather rise above it, abhor it, and cast it away so that we may

---

2. Mariam Bewardi, personal correspondence with author.

maintain our closeness to God and experience God's love. Here I recall, once again, the words of the I'billin saint, Mariam Bewardi, when she said, "In heaven, you will find all vices forgiven, and you will not find pride among them, and in hell you will find all virtues condemned, but you will not find humility among them." Pride is to focus on material things and selfishness, often to impress others. We then hear the voice: "You fool! This very night you will die! And the things you prepared, whose will they be?"

IT IS NOT GIVING UP SIN BUT RATHER COMPLETELY REJECTING IT

It is not doing God a favor that we concede, as if we have a right to all the previous vices. Rather, it is an epidemic that we must get rid of in order to experience God's love. We cannot worship two masters, God and money (Matt 6:24). We must remember that we are transient on this earth, that we do not have a permanent city on earth, and that what we have is what God has entrusted in our hands so that we can invest it, that is, to grow it so that we can help each other in order that human life becomes humane for all people. God, the Almighty, does not expect us to live like angels who have no body. Rather, God expects us to live like human beings, entrusted with creation and its bounties. When the appointed time arrived, God was incarnated through the virgin Mary and took the form of a human being in order to return humans to their original and intended selves, to lift up the image of God in us so there is no longer any place for the Roman proverb, "Man is a wolf to his fellow man (*Homo Hominis Lupus*)."

In fact, in the eyes of Christ, the orientation toward others is different. Humans are created in the image of God, and they should care about salvation for their brothers and sisters. The image is noble, just as the person it represents is generous and a source of dignity. It was Augustine in the *Confessions* who said, "O Lord, our heart will not rest until it rests in Your heart." We do not have a permanent city on earth. Our goal is to return—a true return—to heaven, a return to paradise under the wings of the Creator, whose life gave us life. Saint Augustine had tried all the moral vices, selfishness, and the worship of fire, but he did not find comfort in them. Therefore, he wrote in his *Confessions*, "Our heart will not be at rest unless it is at rest in your heart." Vanity of vanities, all is vanity! We came from God and to God we return. Every other direction we make and take is a wrong direction, a flawed direction, and does not lead to God; this is sin. We will not find comfort unless we turn to God, and only in God will we find comfort. We know what God's will is, but the temptations of this world stand before us as a solid barrier to prevent us from heading towards the goal. So, at times, we walk towards the other false god, and how powerful and tempting that false god can be! But there is no god but God. In the end, "Where your treasure is, there your heart will be." If there is no light in you, then there is darkness. How will darkness feel? We will be alone! But it is the fear of the Lord that satisfies us, yet we often worship gods made with hands.

Because of sin, humans are not always governed by God. Our minds and understandings may turn to dark emotions, inclinations, unbridled desires, insatiable eagerness, and the love of possessions. The person rich in worldly things does not sit and remember that he is from dust and to dust he will return sooner or later, and no matter how long the time is, it is near. The rich person may be poor and does not taste true happiness. Therefore, this person will leave everything, all his possessions and children, and against his will, he still lives in time and walks against his will into eternity. Time is fleeting, but eternity is permanent, ever existing. I leave my family, my home, my money, and my wishes in this world and return to dust.

Yet even with this awareness, the temptations of sin may still overcome us, and we go our own way, saying, "Although I see this truth, I do not understand it." It is as if we forget our responsibility before the eternal truth. "Time is transient, but eternity is permanent." Blessed is the person who understands and internalizes this truth and overcomes emotions, pleasures, and the love of possessions and domination, not forgetting that he is sooner or later—and no matter how much later—very near to the day when his soul will be taken from him. He will leave everything and appear before the Creator, for there is no cover except his good deeds, the acts of mercy, forgiveness, and reconciliation. This is Jesus Christ's project on earth: to heal these people and help them understand that the good life, full of happiness and joy, is to be in the arms of the loving God. Our duty and responsibility are clear: to forgive and tolerate, reconcile, and make peace.

God is light, and there is no darkness in God. In the dark, we cannot see our way. Darkness is a characteristic of the night. When people do not know where they are going and to what abyss they are drawn, they walk in darkness. In heaven there is no darkness and there is no night. Yet people still love darkness because their deeds are evil. "Blessed are the meek and pure at heart, for they shall see God" (Matt 5:5).

Often, a person lives life far from God, as if saying, "I enjoy good health, and I have a lot of money. I wish I had more and more money, and I live obsessed with the love of money. I don't need prayer." So, these people deny that God has authority over their lives. In time, they may turn to God, but it may be too late. But God does not give up and wants us to be in excellent health and to live in a spiritual way. God is the God of the living, not the God of the dead. It is impossible to merge darkness with light. "You cannot worship two masters: God and money." We cannot love two contradictory things. Love is absolute; it is either love or not, and the opposite of love is hatred and evil. So, either we love God or serve evil. There is no room for half measures or standing in the middle. "He who does not gather with me, scatters. Whoever is not with me is against me" (Luke 11:23). The absence of love makes us believe in deception: "If you are the Son of God, order this stone to become a loaf of bread." The absence of love makes us resort to stunts. "Throw yourself from the top to the bottom, and everyone will believe in you," but "do not put the Lord, your God, to the test." Finally, the absence of love makes us bow our heads and prostrate ourselves to the Evil One, and thus, we try to obtain happiness by supporting evil and submitting to the Evil One.

Beware of becoming slaves to the good things made by human hands in order to please other people. We become attached to them and become unable to live without them; we become their servants and slaves to them. Our happiness is in their presence and our unhappiness is with their absence. Humans, perhaps even you, dear reader, often surrender yourself to the love of material and earthly things and fall in love with material things. They become the god that a person may worship. In fact, God has given us these good things so that we can use them, provided that our happiness is not exclusively related to their presence and our unhappiness to their absence. It is important to note that even with them, we do not feel joy or happiness. True peace does not come because our heart is full of worldly things and obsessed with earthly things. One who loves God will leave everything behind and move from this false world to the world of honesty, to the world of truth and not where falsehoods are control the situation (Mark 10:21). "Do not lay up for yourselves treasures on earth, where worms eat and destroy everything. Rather, lay up for yourselves treasures in heaven, where neither worms nor moths destroy good things, and no thief can steal" (Matt 6:19). Honesty before and commitment to God will lead to peace and happiness.

An example of attachment to earthly goods is found in the Acts of the Apostles with the story of Hananya and his wife Sappirah. A lie was told about possessions, and there was a confrontation about dishonesty: "You did not lie to people, but to God" (Acts 5:1–11). This reminds us as well of the great challenge that the prophet Elijah issued to the prophets of Baal: "If God is the truth, follow him, and if Baal is God, follow him" (1 Kgs 18:21).

Jesus teaches us not to be anxious in our lives but to have trust in God, for our heavenly Father-mother is taking care of us with care and exemplary parental love! "Look at the birds flying about! They neither plant nor harvest, nor do they gather food into barns; yet your heavenly Father feeds them. Aren't you worth more than they are?" (Matt 6:26). He did not say "their father" but "your father." And you are more important than the birds of the sky and more valuable than the sparrows of the field. He knows that you need your daily bread. Do not worry about trying to increase even one finger on your stature, for your God accepts you as you are and wants you to become what you were created to be. You cannot add any bit to your stature, and do not forget that the hairs on your head are counted, and not a single hair falls from your head except with the permission of God. Take heart, for your loving God loves you, and God will not give you stones if you ask him for bread, nor will he give you thorns if you ask him for grapes.[3] Even when you pray, do not say much. God will not answer you through your many words. But when you pray, go into your room, close the door, and pray to your loving God who sees in secret, and your God who sees in secret will reward you. And when you pray, say:

Our Father, who art in heaven:[4]

1. Hallowed be thy Name;
2. Thy kingdom come,
3. Thy will be done on Earth, as it is in heaven.
4. Give us this day our daily bread
5. and forgive us our trespasses, as we forgive those who trespass against us.
6. And lead us not into temptation, but deliver us from evil.
7. For thine is the kingdom, the power, and the glory, for ever and ever.

This is a declaration of faith that asserts that God is able to grant us our requests, and that God can help us overcome our unruly tendencies. The world is God's domain, and the power is in God's hand, and the glory, all the glory, as well as the might, all the might, belong to God forever.

---

3. Again, this passage "invites" the description of the loving care of a parent. It is also the case in reference to the classic prayers that begin with "Our Father."

4. This prayer is a great confession. We pray as we acknowledge that the One to whom we are praying is the loving Parent of the human family.

THE RICH IS THE ONE WHO CLINGS TO THE PLEASURES OF THIS LIFE

In reality, Satan does not care about the extent of a person's attachment to money as much as he cares about the person's attachment to the goods of this world, to worldly things.[5] The attachment to something other than God is sufficient for Satan, who will entangle a person and distance the person from God. This is what Satan wants: for us to turn away from God no matter the direction because where our heart is, there our treasure is. The evil one has very tempting methods. But because he is truly the Son of God, Jesus did not need to prove that he is indeed the Son of God in order to answer Satan's temptation or his commands, as if showing doubt that he is the Son of God and needed to prove to Satan that he is truly the Son of God. "If you are the Son of God"! Does Jesus really need to prove that he is the Son of God? Satan knows that Christ is the Son of God. So, his challenge to Jesus, "If you are the Son of God," is insolence and an attempt to make Jesus agree with the malicious tempter. Then the Lord said to him, "Behind me, Satan." That is, hide yourself, Satan. In response to the first temptation, God answered, "Do not tempt the Lord your God, for man does not live by bread alone" (Luke 4:12).

God is the giver of life and gave it to us out of great love, not by merit on our part. God does not mess with people's lives. God gifted it and God takes care of it. The hairs on your head are counted, and not a hair on your head will fall without the will of your loving God in heaven. We rely on God, and God takes care of us and cares for us on our journey towards the reign of God, that is, on our path of returning to our Creator. We are better than the birds of the sky and the animals of the field. Yes, God takes care of them, but we, you and I, my brother or sister, should not forget that God created us in the divine image and likeness. He created us better than the angels and became enfleshed from a woman, the virgin Mary. God loved us so much that God sent his beloved Son so that everyone who believes in him might have life. Do not

---

5. The reference to Satan is one way of speaking about the forces of evil.

worry, do not be upset, and do not doubt the great love of God for us. God cares for us, feeds us, and showers us with divine goodness so that we can enjoy what has been given and share with each other our gratitude of God's goodness. Being so blessed, we do not say to ourselves, "These bounties are mine, and no one has any right to share them with me." If we say these words, God has prepared for us the answer: "You fool, your life may be taken from you tonight." That which you gathered and refrained from sharing with your hungry and naked fellow humans was a gift to be shared. For whom will you leave all this, and why? It is how we used and stored these possessions that will be judged by the Creator. It is how you manage what you have that decides your fate.

GOD CARES FOR US THROUGH HIS MERCY AND LOVE

Isn't it remarkable how Jesus Christ gave us the example of the birds of the sky and the foxes of the field, which neither sow nor reap, and yet your heavenly Father feeds them? He did not say "their Father" but rather "your heavenly Father." This means that it is our duty and our responsibility to care about what belongs to God and not to be troubled, worried, or anxious about what to eat or what to wear. Our loving God cares about the life, food, and drink of birds in the wild, and even cares more about us, the children of God. Do not worry about what you will eat or what you will drink. Consider the birds of the sky and the beasts of the field, for God protects them and takes care of them, and even more for you, you of little faith. Seek first the reign of God, and all this will be added to you.

I conclude my reflections with what I read on the gravestone of a rich man who asked for the following to be written on his headstone: "Everything I gave during my life, I found on the day I died, and everything I was attached to during my life, I lost on the day I died. Whoever has ears to hear, let him hear."

CHAPTER FOUR

On Living the Teachings of the Sermon on the Mount

"In everything do to others as you would have them do to you; for this is the law and the prophets."

(MATT 7:12)

CHRIST IS THE COMPLETION OF THE LAW AND SEAL OF THE PROPHETS

WE HAVE BEEN WRITING about and learning from the One who "fulfills" the prophecies and the teachings about the law. It has become clear to us that we cannot understand the personality of Jesus Christ in isolation from his people and their traditions, from the law of the Jewish faith, and from the religious rituals in which the Savior was raised and nurtured from an early age. He had been living with the God, his loving guide, since and even before his childhood, and Christ was with God who existed before anything existed that was brought into being (John 1:1–3). This is the reason that when Jesus was with his parents in Jerusalem as a boy, he answered Mary and Joseph with a question: "Why do you seek me?" His question implies that they should have known where he was. So, he replies, "Why do you look for me? Don't you know that I have to be concerned with God's affairs?" (Luke 2:41–51). In other words, he explains that of course he should be in the temple talking with the elders and not lost![1] It is Jesus who gave us the Beatitudes.

If we ponder the Beatitudes in Matt 5–7, we notice that they are the credentials of every Christian, just as they are fully present in the Nazarene, Jesus Christ.

1. He was the one poor in spirit, even as a boy, because he longed for time to reflect and wonder, and he had many questions. He needed to commune with God and find answers.

2. He was among those weeping for Lazarus, for the son of the widow from Nain, and for Jerusalem. He was the one who said to the disciples before his arrest, "I have longed to eat this Passover with you, and I tell you that I will not eat it again, until we eat it in the kingdom of heaven" (John 22:7–13).

3. He was the one saddened about the rich young man clinging to his money because he did not worship God but money, and he saw so many who were poor and sick.

4. He was the one who was meek during his life on earth in Galilee. He took a child, embraced him and said, "Unless you all return and become like children, you will not enter the kingdom of heaven" (Matt 22:13–15). He, as a humble teacher and prophet, sought a more just society, which is the foundation for peace.

5. He was the one who hungered and thirsted for righteousness and taught us to "do unto others what you want others to do unto you" (Matt 7:12). He reminded his listeners that the way in which you judge others will be used to judge you, and it may be a more severe judgment. He said we should not judge others in harsh ways and urged us to be kind to others and give them grace. He was the one who said, "Give to Caesar

---

1. In this section, I have not always provided the place in the New Testament where these words appear, but the sentences do appear in more than one Gospel as the accounts of the life of Jesus.

what is Caesar's, and to God what is God's" (Matt 22:21), clarifying our understanding of and need for government. Jesus often goes beyond the justice of governments to mercy, and he always helped people to understand. He never broke a fragile reed nor extinguished a dim light: he opened the eyes of humankind.

6. He was mercy personified, and he did not condemn the adulterous woman. He asked, "Where is the adulterous man, or men?" Why were they not there when one of them tested Jesus and questioned his actions? It was not their zeal for the law; they wanted to test Jesus and maybe get him in trouble. Jesus was the one who directed his words to the scribes, the Pharisees, and all those who came to test him. Would he forgive or judge this poor, sinful woman? He challenged them: "He who is without sin among you, let him cast the first stone." Then they began to withdraw, starting with their eldest, one by one. He then raised his eyes and looked at the poor woman and said to her, "Woman, where are your accusers? Has no one judged you?" None of these people judged her, because they could not claim that they were without sin or that they had the right to throw the first stone at this poor woman (John 8:1–11). Whoever considers themselves, according to the Talmud, without sin (and considers themselves perfect when there is no one perfect except God) will be sentenced because of their pride. They withdrew owing to the scale of their hypocrisy, fearing for their safety, and not because they feared God or admitted their sin. Jesus simply did not judge the poor woman.

7. He gave forgiveness, saying, "Neither do I condemn you. Now go, and sin no more" (John 8:11). He was the one who reassured Peter and his followers: "I have prayed for you, and when you go back, strengthen your brothers and sisters." "I did not come to call the righteous but the sinners to repent" (Luke 5:32). He was the one who forgave much of the debtor's debt, that debtor who, upon leaving his master, met with another slave who had owed him fifty dinars. But he did not forgive him his debt, as

the master had forgiven him, being a slave drowning in debt. So, his master said to him, "Shouldn't you have had pity on your brother, just as I had pity on you?" He taught that we are to love others as we love ourselves (Matt 20:24–28).

8. Jesus was pure in heart. He had integrity. Who was as pure in heart as Jesus? It is impossible to find a person as pure-hearted as him. This purity in Jesus was reflected in his concern for peace; he is called the Prince of Peace. He did not just contemplate the beauty of peace but rather lived it, built it, and got his hands dirty creating peace. He was pure in his love for others and longed to create a just society that would bring peace. His integrity and purity in heart was present when he was in the temple and observed the way people worshiped in the temple. He never wavered on these concerns: peace to give security to his people and a temple for them to nurture their spiritual lives. Jesus cared so much about these concerns, never wavering in his commitment, that it contributed to his arrest and ultimate death. Even there, we see his integrity. While he was on the cross, we hear him pray: "Father, forgive them, for they do not know what they do" (Luke 23:34). He freely gave his own blood for love and truth, and these values were who he was as he died.

He was pure at heart even to the point of what one might call naivete as he prays, "Father, forgive them, for they do not know what they do." Jesus did not just teach peace and love but also lived peace and love. He is the Prince of Peace for which the angels sang to the shepherds, "Glory to God in the highest, and on earth peace, and to people joy" (Luke 2:14). He came to wipe away every tear from every eye. He laid a foundation to give to his disciples. He did not spend time contemplating the beauty of peace, but rather, he lived to make peace, getting his hands dirty by doing the hard work building peace and creating a context of love.

His integrity with values became visible on several occasions. For example, he did not hesitate to heal the paralytic on the Sabbath, which aroused the anger of the scribes and

Pharisees. He made the meaning and value of the Sabbath clear to them: "The Sabbath was created for man, not man for the Sabbath" (Mark 2:27). This further infuriated the scribes and Pharisees. Nevertheless, while on the cross, he did not hesitate to appeal to his heavenly Father: "Father, forgive them, for they do not know what they do." Peace be upon him! He was filled with love and lived it in the most demanding of circumstances. He reminded those he heard him speak that there should be no hypocrisy as we speak! Our words should be clear and honest (a "Yes" a "Yes" and "No" a "No").

9. He was truly the Prince of Peace. He said to his disciples after his resurrection, "Peace be to you. My peace I give to you. I do not give it to you as the world gives it" (John 14:27). He spoke to them directly: "Do not worry about what you will eat or what you will drink or what you will wear. Seek first the kingdom of heaven, and all these things will be added to you from your Father who is in heaven" (Matt 6:33).[2] How many times did he heal a sick person, or free an epileptic from his seizures, or heal a blind man, or cleanse a leper? He said, "Come to me, all who are weary, and I will give you rest" (Matt 11:28). Who was more tired than the thief on the cross when he said to Jesus, "Lord, remember me when you come into your kingdom"? Did he not say to this thief on the right, "Truly, I say to you, on this day, you will be with me in Paradise" (Matt 27:38–44). Before that, he was the one who said to the bleeding woman, "Your faith has saved you, so go in peace." He was the one who declared that he did not find faith in Israel like the faith of the Roman commander even though the soldier represented the brutal occupying authority. So, he said to him, "Your daughter has been healed." He looked at the crowd and said to them: "I have not found such faith, no, not even in Israel." He did not hesitate to affirm that God was able to raise up children for Abraham from stones, from every context (Mark 5:34).

---

2. Again, I am using the masculine word "Father" in that it captures the intimacy which Jesus felt with God.

10. Jesus was the one who was persecuted and had all kinds of evil things said about him and against him "falsely, for my sake." Yet he never lost sight of his love and his dedication to the truth. He remained true to the teaching of God. This phrase "falsely, for my sake" shows us who the speaker is. It was God who gave the law to the chosen people. God is the one who liberated them from slavery. God walked before them in the form of a column of fire during the day and light at night. God is the one who parted the sea for the passage of the chosen people and drowned Pharaoh's army. God is the one who said to Moses, "I am": in other words, "Before Abraham was, I existed." Moses did not know God's name but rather told the people that God is the God of their ancestors, Abraham, Isaac, and Jacob, who sent him to them and to Pharaoh. "You are great, O Lord, and your works are marvelous, and no words are sufficient to praise your wonders" (Rev 15:3,).

11. Who was more persecuted for the sake of justice and for the sake of righteousness than Jesus Christ? Why did the people of Nazareth attempt to throw him down from the top of the mountain, where their city was built, if not for their lack of faith, which made him leave Nazareth and take refuge in Capernaum? In how many events do we see the Son of Mary persecuted for the sake of righteousness? He was born persecuted, as his mother had no place to stay, so she took refuge in a cave near Bethlehem, and no sooner was he born a child than he became a cause of disagreement or a stumbling block in front of many powerful people of this world. So, they plotted against him and told lies about him in order to bring him down to the pit of destruction (see Isa 53:1–5; 61:1–2). Yet he prevailed. "The Spirit of the Lord is upon me, because he has anointed me to preach good news to the poor. He has sent me to proclaim release to the captives and recovering of sight to the blind, to set at liberty those who are oppressed, to proclaim the acceptable year of the Lord" (Luke 4:18–19).

"You go, and when you find the child, come and tell me, so that I may also go and worship him" (Matt 2:8). How foolish you were, Herod! Did you want to deceive the wise men who, at the inspiration of God, came from afar? No, you would not succeed. When the magi met the newborn, they presented to him what is offered to kings, to humankind, and to God, and they returned to their country through a new path. Their lives were renewed, and they left the spiteful, foolish Herod waiting. Thus, the child and his mother, Mary, and righteous Joseph were forced to take refuge in Egypt, because his hour had not yet come. They took refuge in Egypt understanding that "the Lord is my shepherd, Whom shall I fear? The Lord is my soul's guard. Whom shall I fear?" (Ps 23:1–2).

They took refuge in Egypt, just as many years before another man did who had been sold by his brothers to the Ishmaelites and took refuge there: Joseph the righteous. There were parallels in the two stories, as Joseph, who later became a symbol of Christ, saved his people from famine, and Jesus saved the world from sin and evil. The stone that the builders rejected has become the cornerstone. The Lord has done this, and it is marvelous in our eyes.

THE BEATITUDES CHARACTERIZE THE LIFE OF JESUS

These Beatitudes are what Saint Matthew understood to be descriptions of the awaited messiah. It is relatively easy to replace the word "blessed" with the word "Jesus," and thus we get a distinctive and true picture of Jesus, the son of Mary of Nazareth. The following is what we get with this new reading:

- Jesus is the one poor in spirit; therefore, his heart is open to the reign of God.
- Jesus is the sad one; therefore, he will be comforted. We read this in the text of Isaiah, describing the suffering servant and Jesus as the one whom God comforts.

- Jesus is pure in heart; therefore, he sees God like a child because in their innocence, they see God.

- Jesus is the peacemaker, the one who lives peace and the one who builds peace. He has given his entire body, not just his hands, to build peace. At this moment in human history, we need to turn to the one who gives the world peace. The peace that the Lord gives does not come from this world; it is peace that comes from within, and with God's grace, we experience internal peace. We then move into the world to create peace. This peace which the Lord gives empowers us to be concerned about the peace of a ceasefire and the peace of a truce between two armies.[3] God's peace begins from within the person and then becomes the peace of helping others to turn away from evil and war. So, "if your brother forces you to go one mile, go with him two miles, and if he takes your shirt, give him your cloak as well" (Matt 5:40–41). Forgive us our trespasses as we forgive those who trespass against us. The peace of Christ does not deny the enemy, an external force, but first it is peace from within the heart. Since the goal and desire is good and sincere relationships, we express our peace so that the enemy can become a friend. Look at your brother and sister and say to yourself, "I am looking at the most beautiful thing God has created." Thus, through the deep peace we have within us, the enemy becomes the target of reconciliation. With the peace of God written our hears, we invite all others to be our brothers and sisters.

The peace of Christ is the peace that is present when we encounter the other. It is as if we are meeting our beloved one who has been separated from us for a long time. We become the father towards the prodigal son who split his father's money and split his father's heart as well. The father is eagerly waiting for his son to return. Let him return as he is. It does not matter what he did, or what his economic, social, or moral condition is. Just let him return. The father is just waiting for him to return, no matter what signs of degradation

---

3. I write at the time of the great conflict in Gaza and the Middle East.

appear in him. Let him return, and even if he is dead, I will resurrect him. And if he is lost, I will reveal the way to him, not to anywhere but to the merciful and unconditional loving heart of God. Simply come back, and I will purify him as if with hyssop, and I will purify him bright as snow; just let him come back. I love him and I don't want him far from me, so just let him come back. Jesus is the source of peace and the builder of peace, so he is called the Son of God. He says, "My peace I give to you, I do not give it as the world gives it" (John 14:27). We learn from Jesus.

- Jesus is the one they persecuted and had all kinds of evil things said about him falsely. In fact, we might ask what have they not accused him of, or what falsehoods have they not said about him? It is the Evil One, an infidel, a transgressor of the law, which is why he can cast out the evil presence in the persons whom he meets. Those who listened to him did not want to understand that a house divided against itself would be destroyed. They claimed that he was a sinner and that he ate with sinners. He said in return, "Today salvation has come to this house" (Luke 19:9), that is, the house of Zacchaeus the tax collector. He was disobedient, and Jesus helped him become a child of God.

- Jesus might be thought of as a rebel. For example, he claimed that he had the capacity to destroy the temple and rebuild it in three days. They did not recognize him and placed the moral accusations on his pure head. He was like a lamb led to the slaughter, a lamb that had not resisted. Therefore, his life was taken, and he was cast out with sinners.

- There was no one to defend him, not even Peter, who renounced him three times after he claimed that he was ready to go with him even to death if necessary. Peter renounced him for fear that the slave girl might reveal who was and then betrayed him three times even after the resurrection. In the face of the council's threats and those of Nero, Peter fled to Rome for fear of staying and being put to death in Jerusalem. Jesus even appeared to Peter while he was fleeing, and Peter said to him, "*Quo vadis*" (that is, "Where are you going?")? The Master replied, "I am going to be crucified in your place; they seek my life to destroy it." Peter understood, and in his fear and weakness, he returned to Rome where he presented himself as a witness to the truth of Christ. Peter understood that the enemy would crucify him, head down and feet up, a method used by the Romans. But he glorified God in his death and died as a martyr, bearing witness that Christ is the Son of God (Acts 10).

- Jesus is the one who deserved to be with God in heaven. He suffered for us and heard the officials say all kinds of evil things about him falsely. This, too, is how they persecuted the prophets who preceded him. "O Jerusalem, Jerusalem, killing the prophets and stoning those who are sent to you! How often would I have gathered your children together as a hen gathers her brood under her wings, and you would not! Behold, your house is forsaken and desolate" (Matt 23:37–38). Therefore, as in the manger, we see the bull and the donkey on either side of the newborn child to remind us that the donkey knew its owner and the bull knew its feeder, but Israel did not know the Lord God. Poor Israel, its own enemy, its own killer; it calls good evil and evil good. How can those in Israel abandon the spirit of rebellion and denial and actually join the manger, where a Savior was born unto us, who is Christ, the Son of God?

- Jesus is the one who hungers and thirsts for righteousness. He seeks justice. He is the one who did not yield to Satan's evil temptations. Blessed are those who hunger and thirst for righteousness, for they will be filled. "Render to Caesar the things that are Caesar's, and to God the things that are God's" (Mark 12:17). Also, "Let what you say be simply 'Yes' or 'No'; anything more than this comes from evil" (Matt 5:37).

We understand that the Beatitudes express the character of Jesus Christ, and they are descriptions of his life and confirmation of his credentials, as stated in the reading of Isaiah in the temple in Nazareth: "He was despised and rejected by men; a man of sorrows, and acquainted with grief; and as one from whom men hide their faces he was despised, and we esteemed him not. Surely he has borne our griefs and carried our sorrows; yet we esteemed him stricken smitten by God, and afflicted. But he was wounded for our transgressions, he was bruised for our iniquities; upon him was the chastisement that made us whole, and with his stripes we are healed" (Isa 53:3–5). And he also gave confirmation in his answer to the messengers who had imprisoned John, asking on John's behalf, "Are you he who is to come, or shall we look for another?" (Matt 11:3).

If we believe that Jesus is the expected messiah, as he was described by the prophets in the Hebrew Bible, then we understand the importance of what is mentioned in the Gospel of Matthew. Immediately after the Beatitudes, he spoke to the disciples, saying, "You are the salt of the earth" (Matt 5:13). It means that you are the salt of the whole universe, but first of all, you are the salt of the earth where you live. You are the salt of the earth! If salt loses its saltiness, how can the earth be salted? It is then not good for anything, so it gets thrown outside and trampled on by people.

With God present in your life, you are also the light of the world. We are asked to let light spread over all and include all. We also must understand that the light does not belong to us. We read that God makes his sun rise on the righteous and on the evil, and he sends his rain down on the good ear of wheat and on the weed. One of the features of the divine light is that it has revealed and will continue to reveal the way for those traveling in the direction of God, searching and looking for God.

Have confidence in God, that in Jesus we can overcome the evil in the world. This is what was brought to us by Christ's call to the disciples, that they too should be perfect, just as their heavenly Parent is perfect. Just as the Beatitudes are characteristics and virtues of Christ, they must be the credentials of the Christian. We know that the Teacher was persecuted, and just as they persecuted the Teacher, they will persecute the disciple. The prophets were all persecuted in the name of God and for proclaiming the will of God. Likewise, Christians are persecuted for Christ's sake. The prophets were persecuted because of their belief in God. God is the lawgiver and the one who appeared to Moses in the burning bush in Sinai, and God revealed the divine name to him: "I am, I exist." We trust the God of Moses!

YOU ARE THE SALT OF THE EARTH

Christ is the salt of the earth and of the whole world. That is, he gives flavor and seasoning to human life. Christ is the one who carries a message, who was given a mission, a calling with a message for the world, not just for a specific people nor for a particular tribe, for he came to call for unity among all of God's dispersed children. He came to destroy the walls separating peoples. He then cautions his listeners and says that those who believe in Jesus Christ only in words are like chameleons with no original color or personality; they take the color of their environment. He, however, knew where he came from and where he was going, so he refused to conceal himself with the magician's colors. He did not come to enchant anyone, no matter who they were, nor did he hide his true identity as the Savior, the Son of God. We will see that he could have performed this kind of magic, but he did not do anything for his own benefit. We read about him turning water into wine and later turning the wine into his blood and the bread into his body. He did not hesitate to multiply the loaves of bread to feed the people who came to hear him so that they would not get feeble away from home. He turned the five loaves into so much bread that he fed the five thousand and had twelve basketfuls left over of broken bread pieces.

He did not come to perform acrobatic miracles or to dazzle the minds of the people around him, nor did he come to rob them of their free will so that they might follow him as slaves. He gives freedom and does not enslave the free. He multiplied the loaves of bread for those who listened to him all day long. He fed them so that their strength would not fail them. Then he withdrew when they wanted to make him king, because that was not his calling. His calling was to teach them about God's love. They would discover that God truly loves them as they "ate the bread" which he had given to them and became satisfied. He dissociated himself from becoming a human king, and he taught them that "humans do not live on bread alone" but by every word that comes from the mouth of God. Did he not say to his disciples, "Consider the lilies of the field, how they grow and blossom, and Solomon in all his splendor was not dressed like one of them. Consider the birds of the sky, for they neither sow nor reap nor store in barns, but your heavenly Father provides for them. You are better than them all. Seek first the kingdom of heaven, the reign of God, and this righteousness will be given to you" (Matt 6:28–33)?

CHRIST IS THE SALT OF THE EARTH

We also read that "you are the salt of the earth," so be vigilant lest you lose your saltiness and become unable to bring good taste into the world. Then the Creator will say to you, "I know your works: you are neither cold nor hot. Would that you were cold or hot! So, because you are lukewarm, and neither cold nor hot, I will spew you out of my mouth" (Rev 3:15–16). In order for us to maintain our mission and responsibility to serve, we must maintain the fervor of our faith and return to God with repentance. You are the salt of the earth, so do not hide your saltiness and the ability to enrich your relationships. Otherwise, if you lose your saltiness or if you hide out of concern for your life, then your salt is not good for anything except to be thrown out and trampled by people. Salt is vital to food, and you as a disciple are vital to humanity. Without you, humanity will remain in darkness and will continue to regress back to the pride of Babel. Their tongues will become confused, wars will spread, people will become arrogant and self-centered, brother will kill his brother and sister, and humans will become once again a wolf that attacks fellow humans.

Your salt or loving spirit should be a light directed to the world. And your light, the light of God, must be directed to the entire world. God shines the sun on both the righteous and the unrighteous, and Jesus understands that this is his message: "I have come to gather the scattered children of God." Christ is the light of the world, and it is the responsibility of the Christian to be a light to the world, that is, to guide everyone to the love of God. Light opens the way and helps people avoid falling into darkness. Those who walk in the light will be spared the pitfalls and mistakes in their choices and will not fall into darkness. A Christian is a person who declares their faith, who declares who their teacher is, and that "Christ must grow larger, and the Christian must get smaller" (see John 3:30) and not the other way around. It is not with many words that we bring light and salt to the world but with the sincerity and intensity of our actions. "You are the light of the world" (Matt 5:14). Wasn't Christ the light of the world? So, whoever follows him does not walk in darkness. The light must remain gentle and not so bright that it glares so that people won't be afraid and can see the way. Christ's call is not to be a bright light that blinds the eyes. Rather, the light is placed on a lamp in a high place so that people can see the way, continue their journey of following the light, and glorify their God in heaven. How beautiful is the lamp on the lampstand!

It is the farthest from a bright light that blinds the eyes and does not reveal the path. It is not the Christian's responsibility to blind people's eyes with the brightness of his light. The strong, boastful, and arrogant light is like darkness, blinding the eyes, so people remain standing, staring at the light and not following their path to God. Thus, if a person becomes a god to his fellow human being, this person will suffer the fate of the butterfly. The light dazzles the butterfly and attracts it, so it approaches it and gets burned. Likewise, if a Christian does not have a humble light that guides people and points to the path of God, then people will stray and will not follow the path but rather remain only astonished by the light and will not reach the goal.

THE TRUE CHRISTIAN IS THE LIGHT OF THE WORLD

You are the light of the world; you are the ones who lead people to God and not to themselves. "He should grow larger, and we should get smaller." The light that Christ spoke about is a gentle light that illuminates the path and does not blind the eyes of those who see it; so, they are able to continue their journey to God. The light of the Lord Christ reveals the way for people and leads them farther ahead to enlightenment by the Lord's teachings and on an in-depth journey. "Anyone who has seen me, has seen the Father" (John 14:9), and whoever wants to follow Christ, the one who guides us to God, must accept his limitations and life values—that is, carry his cross and follow Christ, as Paul did when he cried out from the depths of his being, "Woe to me if I do not preach of Christ. For I am resolved to know nothing except Jesus Christ, and Him crucified" (1 Cor 9:16).

Paul's preaching of Christ kept him humble, much like other human beings. There was a painful thorn in his body from which he asked God three times to free him, and God's answer was the same answer that he gives us. Facing the thorns of our flesh, God Almighty says to us, "My grace is sufficient for you" (see 2 Cor 12:9). God's grace must be sufficient for the Christian, as it was for Paul. The Christian knows how to thank God in good times and in bad times. So let a weakness or a physical thorn be a cross that one carries following Christ. He comforts us and says, "My grace is sufficient for you!" We must let the thorn of our body and the challenges in our life be carried with gratitude for the blessings God has given us. "My grace is sufficient for you."

What then is a true Christian afraid of? Is he or she afraid of death? Our faith teaches us that the sting of death has been broken. Is the Christian afraid of hell? No, because God has received us in love, and we have been taught how to live by Jesus. Of what then should we be afraid? We need not fear. Those who have been imprisoned have been set free. Yet most us still remain anxious.

What or whom are you afraid of, my brother, and you, my sister? From aging and from death? Are you afraid of a disease that has befallen your body, or another thorn that has entered your skin and burrowed there? Don't be shortsighted and consumed by fear. We learn from Jesus that the cross and suffering lasted for three days, after which the dawn of resurrection emerged. Jesus followed in faith, with patience, and the resurrection of Easter came. Be patient, for he who is patient to the end will be saved. You want salvation, so be patient, carry your cross, and follow Christ. When he rises, he lifts everyone up to him, so he rises and raises you up, and nothing remains on the cross but your sins.

We see Jesus's credentials on his visit to the temple in Nazareth: "The Spirit of the Lord is on me, because he has anointed me to proclaim the good news to the poor. He has sent me to proclaim freedom for the prisoners, and recovery of sight for the blind, to set the oppressed free, and proclaim the year of the Lord's favor" (Luke 4:18–19).

We see confirmation of the "credentials" of Jesus in the answer that he gave to the disciples about the imprisoned John, whom he, their teacher (John the Baptist), sent to ask Jesus, "Are you the one who is going to come, or should we expect someone else?" Jesus answered them, saying, "Go back and tell John what you have seen and heard. The blind receive sight, the lame walk, those who have leprosy are cleansed, the deaf hear, the dead are raised, and the good news is proclaimed to the poor; blessed is he who does not doubt me. Blessed is anyone who does not stumble on account of me" (Luke 7:18–23). These are the comforting words of Jesus, the Messiah, and he is the fulfillment of the law and the prophets.

YOU WHO WERE BAPTIZED INTO CHRIST AND HAVE CLOTHED YOURSELVES WITH CHRIST

We have said that the Beatitudes are the credentials of the true Christian. They represent assurance that the Christian's credentials are real. We underline that the Christian's life will call on us to carry our crosses and follow Christ in the path that Christ chose. We find comfort that the end of the life of Jesus on earth was resurrection and the ascension to heaven. But we know the path we must follow first is on earth. It passes through the passion, ending initially with the cross, and later comes the resurrection.

This will be our journey. We cannot ignore the intermediary stations. Many people want to cross directly from Palm Sunday to

Resurrection Sunday and leave behind all the stations in between of the Holy Week: the crucifixion and the grave. But how can there be resurrection without death, even when death is unpleasant and painful? If Christ did not die, there would be no resurrection, and if Christ did not rise, then our faith is invalid, and we are the most miserable people. But he rose! Truly, he has risen! He broke the sting of death and shattered the threats of hell, and he reminds us, "He who is patient to the end will be saved" (Matt 24:13).

Jesus waited patiently until the end, until everything was accomplished; then he passed away. We must follow Christ during the Holy Week in order to be alert to receive the bridegroom and be blessed to receive the washing of the feet, the sacrament of priesthood, and the Eucharist. It is necessary to accompany Christ on the way of the cross, on the way of our cross, before the resurrection.

We remember that Jesus Christ announced his credentials to those present at the Nazareth temple: "The Spirit of the Lord is on me, because he has anointed me to proclaim good news to the poor. He has sent me to proclaim freedom for the prisoners, and recovery of sight for the blind, to set the oppressed free, to proclaim the year of the Lord's favor" (Luke 4:18). Then he closed the book and returned it to the servant and sat down.

The details of his life are demonstrated in the Beatitudes, and the Christian's credentials are to seek to live and be true to the Beatitudes, as he was. We read about his life in the Sermon on the Mount and ask the Holy Spirit to enlighten us and guide our steps. God is the one who grants understanding and empowers us to follow the path of Jesus.

CHAPTER FIVE

Sermon on the Mount: The Pathway to God

"Truly I tell you, wherever this good news is proclaimed in the whole world, what she has done will be told in remembrance of her."

(MATT 26:13)

MY GRACE IS SUFFICIENT FOR YOU: OVERCOME PAST MISTAKES AND MOVE FORWARD

I still have several topics that I want to write about, provided God gives me the gift of life and the gift of memory. I want to share while there is still ample time. My range of experiences in my many travels has filled my mind and heart, and I would like to have some of these insights to be recorded for future generations. The story of Mar Elias Educational Institutions deserves to be written in a book of its own in order to enlighten future generations, especially the graduates of these institutions, all of whom are my beloved children.

Sermon on the Mount: The Pathway to God

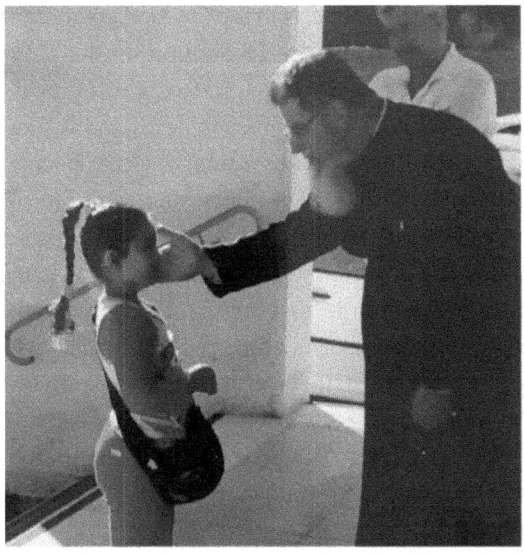

Let the little children come to me, and do not hinder them

I feel an urgent desire to move on to where my Lord is, and I wish, at the same time, that my life would continue so that I may continue to be a servant in the church. I do want to continue my work here on earth, which is God's field. And let no doubter think that there is contradiction in my words; my zeal for Christ and his cause in the world is greater than ever, and woe to me if I do not preach the good news of Christ. But I fear that this goal may not be achieved because there are some who do not easily forgive and continue to oppose me. They are still present, and they hold in their hands the way our church in Galilee should function and carry out its mission. But the message of Christ, the one who was crucified for our benefit, should be the primary concern and guide. The church will be much more in keeping with God's will for its future if we can move beyond any mistakes I may have made. The church should not be distracted by this moment in the past. In keeping with this goal, I would like to review the ways that I have tried to live the values of the Sermon on the Mount, experiencing forgiveness and seeking to follow God's will and way.

The first step, of course, is to seek to be clear about the meaning of the teaching of Jesus in the Sermon on the Mount. It was most likely more than one sermon. In fact, it was probably several sermons and teaching lectures given by Jesus. In his time, without newspapers and electronic recording devices, people remembered what was said by repeating it several times to others who were not present and wanted to use the truth of his teaching in other settings and new congregations. There was an extensive oral tradition, very common in that culture, that preserved what had been taught for the good of all of the people, many of whom could not be present. We have, then, in the Sermon on the Mount the wonderful teaching of Jesus, carefully remembered by those who functioned as scribes and passed on the teaching in oral form. It was a way of life for them, and we still have traces of this pattern of communication.

Christ rose on the cross, died, and rose again, and he continues to forgive. Christ does not need my help in spreading his reign as the Lord of the church. Yet I continue to hear the divine voice calling. He says to me, "Whoever wants to follow me, let him deny himself, and take up his cross and follow me" (Matt 16:24). We often, in our human and selfish capacity, burden others with our crosses and claim that we follow Christ even if we carry some problems from the past. That same voice tells us that we have to be sure that we are following him with his cross in our hearts and minds. There is the risk that we may bypass him or get ahead of him and then no longer see anything except our own agenda based on our needs. We also know that we have been forgiven! It is time to move on and give full attention to the mission of Jesus. We know, deep in our hearts, that he is the light of our path to God. As we move forward, we must be sure that we see him in front of us and are not be blinded by exclusive attention to the problems of the past and our personal concerns.

We must not forget what Jesus Christ said, and I repeat, "Whoever wants to follow me should deny himself and take up his cross and follow me." So, without carrying our crosses and following Christ, it is impossible for us to achieve the goals which we have in serving Christ. Woe to us if we burden people with concerns that do not advance the program Christ has given to us. We need to "turn the page" on our past, trust in God's forgiveness, and give our full attention to following the will and way of God.

My great wish is for the conflicts and trials within the church to end and for me to be relieved from spending time on the past rather than serving the church in Galilee. It was the forgiven Peter who led the new church and the restored Paul who was the church's first and most trusted missionary. Who knows, perhaps the new bishop will be gifted enough to end the disputes, give everyone their due, and end the period of conflict and settle our accounts. I have moved on from some of my responsibilities at the Mar Elias Institutions and am now ready to give new leadership wherever the need matches my experience and gifts.

God has given me new vision and a deep desire to serve as long as I have ability to do the work that is so urgent. There is so much to learn from my mistakes, and the Bible is filled with those who failed, were forgiven, and then gave great service to the church. It was Peter who became the first bishop of the church in Rome. I pray for the church; it is God's church and God is the one who planted it. We need to move forward together, learning from the past and praying for God's guidance in the future.

My role now is to praise and glorify God at every opportunity. Every day, I repeat many times these prayers: "Holy God, Holy Mighty, Holy Immortal, have mercy on us." Then I repeat the psalm: "Have mercy on me, O God, with your great mercy, and in your great compassion erase my transgressions" (Ps 51:1); "release your servant, according to your word, in peace" (Luke 2:29). I conclude my prayers with these words from Ps 36: "Your love, Lord, reaches to the heavens, your faithfulness to the clouds. Your justice is higher than mountains, your judgment is like the great deep sea. O our God, how formidable is your house! People take refuge under the shade of your wings. They drink from the abundance of your house, for you have the fountain of life. In your light, we see light. Extend your mercy to those who know you. I receive Your mercy with gratitude and hear Your Voice calling me to learn and serve, and to learn and serve is the call to all Christians in the world" (Ps 36:5–7).

A PRAYER WITH MEMBERS OF THE NEOCATECHUMENAL MOVEMENT

Already, some opportunities to serve have become available. Yesterday—and it was a Friday; the date itself is not important—I received an invitation from Father Rino to attend a meeting with the Neocatechumenal Movement in the House of Galilee. I found it difficult to travel to the House of Galilee (Domus Galilaeae) because I no longer feel comfortable driving long distances. So, I apologized for not being able to come for this reason. However, the people in charge at the House of Galilee insisted, saying that they hoped I would come and participate in this meeting, and that they would send a car that will bring me to them and take me back home. I gratefully accepted, and within an hour, the car was in front of the house. At ten o'clock in the morning, we arrived at the House of Galilee.

I was surprised by what I saw. I was expecting a small group to participate in the cohabitation meeting, but I saw more than four hundred people, most of them young people, from all the villages of Galilee, from Jerusalem and its suburbs, and many catechumens from Europe and from the Americas. The auditorium was packed with attendees. They suggested that I preside over the meeting, but I politely refused, saying to them, "I came to pray with you and to be one among you, not to sit in the president's chair." I sat in the audience, and one of the brothers brought me a very comfortable chair, placing it next to me and inviting me to sit in it. I refused and told him, "There is no need for a comfortable chair; I came to be one among you and with you."

The meeting started with readings from the Holy Bible, beginning with the Old Testament and concluding with the New Testament. The whole time I sat in that simple chair, and I got tired and wished the meeting would end. I knew that everything that begins has an end. The meeting paused, so I hurried to lie down.

It was absolutely necessary for me to stretch, even for a few minutes. Then, half an hour later, the meeting commenced, focusing on a passage from the New Testament about how to understand the ways of God. It lasted for two and a half hours. Before dinner, I apologized and asked to be taken home, and the driver accommodated me, but I continued to think about how we speak of God.

The readings were about repentance (*teshuvah* in Hebrew) and returning to God. Father Rino commented that God was the Father of mercies, that is, the most gracious, most merciful, the God of mercy and compassion. The word "repentance" (*teshuvah*), for us as Arabs, is a very important word that references our return to our faith in God after failing in some way. Mercy (*raḥma* in Arabic) reminds us of the womb (*raḥem)* to which we return when we repent. The womb inspires in us feelings of love and tenderness, kindness and warmth, and the joy of acceptance. In order to enjoy God's mercy and to enter God's womb, we must repent (*teshuva*). This is an ordinary word commonly used in the Hebrew language, and it means that we are accepted through repentance if we have committed apostasy. We also "repent" to each other, that is, I will say "I am sorry" to you, and you will say "I am sorry" to me.

God replies, "So, you will be my people, and I will be your God." It means a return to the love of God, to God's mercy, and it is the process of being received by God. We hear the message of God who says, "I want the repentance of the sinner, that is, the salvation of the sinner, and not his or her destruction." We trust our prayer to the Lord our God, the God of Abraham, who forgives us. *Teshuvah* means apostasy and returning to God, to the God of mercies, and as we practice it, we able to return to the mercies of God, to the womb of God. Likewise, the word *davar* in both Hebrew and Aramaic means at the same time "a thing" and "a word." Christ is the word of God, and he is tangible, incarnated, and embodied. It is through him that we are forgiven.

Davar Elohim means the word of God, that part of God which accomplishes the divine purposes. Scholars have discovered that Yahweh, or El, has been the God of the Jews from the time of the prophet Moses, to whom God appeared in the burning bush in Sinai. It is important to note that *Elohim*, as a word for God, is the result of many years in the development of thought about the Creator. Gradually, they (the Hebrew people) began to believe in the God of gods: Elohim, which is a plural form in Hebrew. Every time this word appears in a manuscript in Scripture, the Jews read it to this day as *Adonai*, allowing God to be spoken about in the plural form, the totality of God, the one who is called Jehovah.

Elohim is the God of the universe and the God of creation. Religious Jews do not pronounce the name of the Creator Almighty; they say that God is "the Name, Blessed is He." The unknown God that no one sees is the God of Moses who appeared in the burning bush. Elohim is the God of gods. He is God par excellence and is the Father of our Lord Jesus Christ, who revealed himself to us in the person of Christ as the Father.[1] He is the "heavenly Father" whom we do not address in the singular: O my God, "Father," but rather in the plural, *Abino*, or "our Father who art in heaven." These words and expressions help us understand who Jesus Christ is.

The first session of the cohabitation meeting discussed these thoughts about God and lasted from nine o'clock until half past one o'clock without stopping. Then, after a half-hour break, they continued discussing these ideas about God from two o'clock until eight o'clock, again nonstop. The first session was mostly devoted to examining the Old Testament and seeing in what ways the Hebrew Bible may point to the person of Jesus Christ. Jesus was viewed as the fulfillment of the law and the prophets and was understood as the long-awaited messiah. The Hebrew Bible points to long awaiting the messiah, the One who is the way, the truth, and the life.

These were beautiful spiritual sessions during which we did not feel tired or despondent. We actually wished for them to continue because we felt we were in the company of the humble and gentle-hearted Savior, who was merciful to sinners and loved the righteous. We felt invited to be with the disciples as they waited for

---

1. It is somewhat difficult to avoid all the references to "Father," a masculine reference, but it goes well beyond gender and speaks of God as love and the one who cares for us. On occasion, in our litanies, we say "Father-mother God."

the transfiguration, saying: "Lord, it is good for us to stay here. If you wish, we can set up three tents: one for you, one for Moses, and one for Elijah" (Matt 17:4). Peter assumed that he and his companions would find a special place in the proposed tents and be in the very presence of God.

But every beginning has an end, and every cohabitation has a send-off. The sessions ended with everyone being invited to get up and move around to meet the people. We were told that we were ambassadors for Christ, working in the Lord's field, not just in our own fields. We were invited to invest our talents, which the field owner, the master, has entrusted to us. We were told that we must have a good return; otherwise, if you slacken and neglect your talents, they will be taken from you, and you will be left empty-handed.

CHRIST IS THE FINAL FRUITION OF THE OLD TESTAMENT

In essence, we were told that the only way we can understand fully who Jesus is by referring to the Old Testament. Christ is present in the Old Testament, and that is evident in the fact that he is the fulfillment of the law and the prophets. We then looked to the New Testament and saw how he is the fulfillment of God's promise in the Old Testament. We should not ignore the passages in the Old Testament,[2] for they enable us to understand who Jesus Christ is: the Son of the living God, who did not come to abolish the law and the prophets but rather to fulfill the law and the prophets.[3] We find the cradle of Jesus Christ in the Old Testament and the field in which he grew from the branch of Jesse, as well as where he was taught the customs, traditions, and law found in the Old Testament, which he came to complete, not to abolish. The expression

---

2. There are times when it is wise not to speak about the Old Testament, but to speak of the Hebrew Bible is not to imply that it is old and no longer relevant. Doing so here is to use the language of the gathering.

3. The expression "the law and the prophets" was often a shortened form of speaking about the revelation in the Old Testament.

"to complete" does not mean that it was incomplete, but rather to restore its completeness and true meaning.

One example of this learning was to restore the value of the Sabbath; it was made for man and woman, not man and woman for the Sabbath. Another lesson was to understand how we should love our neighbor, which occasionally lacked its broad meaning and its comprehensiveness in the Hebrew Bible. But Jesus was clear! The neighbor is not just love shared between Jews but rather every human being created in the image and likeness of God. Thus, the closest person to the Jew who fell among the thieves was the merciful Samaritan, and Jesus said, "You go and be like the Samaritan" (Luke 10:37). Be kind, loving, and respectful to your parents, as the Lord commands in the Ten Commandments. Respecting them is much more important than making offerings to God in compensation for not respecting parents. This is what the Lord Christ, glory be to him, meant when he said, "I did not come to abolish the law, but to fulfill it." And this is what he taught in the Sermon on the Mount. He restored authenticity to the law, especially since the scribes and Pharisees distorted the law and made the religious establishment not unlike "a den of thieves."

So, he upended the tables of the money changers and kicked out the animal sellers and declared that the divine temple should be called a house of prayer. We, therefore, conclude that God's love is directed to every human being and to all of creation. As for the scribes and Pharisees, Jesus said that they diminished the full meaning of love and service to God.

It may have served their unimportant goals, especially in relation to the fact that God is the God of mercies. It was possible to return from apostasy and decadence into which they had gone. There was happiness to receive *teshuvah*, meaning the return to the One who created us. It was the Creator who walked with Adam in paradise, until Adam rebelled against God. The first thing Adam became aware of as soon as he rebelled was that he was afraid and naked! He was looking for a place to hide and a way to get rid of the fear. So, he hid from the face of God and started to retreat from God. As for God, the God of love began searching for Adam. "O

Adam, where are you? Why did you hide from my face? Have you eaten from the tree of the knowledge of good and evil?" Humans did not find stability and resorted to hiding because Adam lost his stability. Later, they tried to build the Tower of Babel in order to reach God again. However, with life and work underway, languages became confused. Adam, representing humankind, was unable to complete the tower, and he became a stranger to God, a stranger to himself, and even an enemy to himself.

PENTECOST AND THE TOWER OF BABEL

The Day of Pentecost (Greek for "fiftieth day") was the occasion for the outpouring of the Holy Spirit, and one of its most important results was that it called everyone to unity, eliminating the human traditions that divided humanity into Jew and gentile, man and woman, master and slave. This is in contrast to the confusion of tongues and going astray while building the Tower of Babel. Therefore, the coming of the Holy Spirit was a renewed call for humans to wake up and rededicate their lives.

Thanks to the resurrection of Christ, there is no longer favoring, nor preference for a Jew over a gentile, for a man over a woman, nor for a master over a slave since all are called to become children of God by adoption. Neither being circumcised nor uncircumcised saves a person, but rather, faith in Christ saves a person. Christ is the Lord of salvation, and he is available to all, to every man and to every woman. "For you who were baptized into Christ and have clothed yourselves with Christ" (Gal 3:27). The gates of hell have been shattered; the path is open to all. Belief in the resurrection and working to spread the news is what save all people and guide them to heaven, where the company of everyone who was created in the image and likeness of God will be. Therefore, the invitation from God is directed to everyone who is born a child. Praise be to God, people will no longer find themselves lost as they put their faith in the coming of Christ, the one anointed by God, who came to save us from our inflated selves and restore us to humility by confessing our poverty in the presence of God. Jesus came to restore the purity of our hearts and transform us from a weeping creature into a consoled creature, from a sad creature to a joyful one, from a desperate creature to a human being who carries hope and faith and awaits salvation. "You who were baptized into Christ have clothed yourselves with deep faith and able to sing with joy" (Gal 3:27). Hallelujah, praise God.

"GET UP, THERE IS PLENTY TO DO"

God invites us to descend from the mountain of our transfiguration to the society that thirsts for love and the unity of the human family. Come down from your mountain, come out of your isolation, and be a light to the world and the salt of the earth, a miracle to the people and a light to the nations. Jesus came that we might have life and that life will be better for us. The message of Jesus is an invitation to preach the good news to all nations without exception since they are all created babies in the image and with the likeness of God himself. It is strange that the prophet did not say, "Be a light for the people of God and salt for the chosen." Rather, he chose to call everyone to be a light for the people and salt for the nations.

THE CHRISTMAS TREE

On that evening, December 19th, 2019, six days before Christmas, celebrations increased in preparation for Christmas: celebrations at school, in classrooms, in large halls, in the squares, in churches, and in places of worship. Everyone was celebrating and singing "until Jesus arrives, until Jesus arrives." We had the honor of having the Shefa-Amrite Ba'ath Choir (meaning "resurrection"), led by Mr. Raheeb Haddad, hold a Christmas carol concert. The ceremony was wonderful and the hymns were beautiful. There were only two speakers, Professor Simon Khoury at the beginning of the ceremony and I, the bishop, your brother and servant, concluding it. Below is a brief description of how we celebrated.

This was not the first time we had hosted the Ba'ath Choir in this church. At every celebration, I used to tell them that the choir and their beloved maestro had lifted us to heaven. But this time, no, they did not lift us to heaven; rather, they lowered heaven to us, and they created in our hearts feelings of awaiting and anticipation "until Jesus arrives." So, thank you, Ba'ath Choir, for your wonderful, sacred achievement. May God bless you with all goodness. There is no doubt that you know the words of the Holy Fathers (mothers): The chanter prays twice. But now, I tell you without hesitation that you are chanters who pray four hundred times, according to the number of attendees in this church.

"UNTIL JESUS ARRIVES" (*TA YOUSAL YASSOU*)

Celebrations continued at the school, in churches, and in places of worship. Decorated Christmas trees stood in every corner of the institution, so much so that if we collected all the Christmas trees from the school, we would get a large forest. All these celebrations created in us feelings of awaiting and anticipation. What remains is the time for the reception, receiving the One being celebrated, "the transcendent essence, a child, and He is our God before the ages" (see John 1). Our Father who art in heaven, may your will be done on earth as it is in heaven. Give us our daily bread. The bread, without which we cannot live, comes from wheat. The Arabic word for "wheat" is made up of the three letters *qmh* and is pronounced *qamḥ*. If these letters do not combine, they will remain dead letters, and we will die of hunger, because we will have no wheat! From our wheat, we have our daily bread, and when the letters are united, we have what we desire: God's will "on earth as it is in heaven" will materialize. The three letters in *qamḥ*, the Arabic word for "wheat," can be interpreted as follows:

> Let **Q** be the first letter in the Arabic word "Qorban," symbolizing Eid Al-Adha in Islam.
>
> Let **M** be the first letter in the Arabic word "Milad," symbolizing glorious Christmas in Christianity.

And let **H** be the first letter in the word "Hanukkah," symbolizing the Festival of Lights in Judaism.

So, with the letters combined together, we get wheat, and thus the law becomes feasible. Otherwise, woe to us if we follow the path of the politicians and warlords. They have no wheat and no law for their transactions. They call what is wrong good, and what is evil they call good. War becomes peace; brutality, killing, and destruction become heroism; and the confiscation of land and country is called heroism and victory. That is how whatever you want can be called the opposite, but that is not the will of God. We have made the relative a stranger (gentile); that is, what we do not see, we call the other, standing behind, so we do not see him. The Arabic word for "other" is *akhar*, so with humility, I suggest that we delete the letters "a" and "r" so that the word becomes *akh*, which means "brother" in Arabic, not another unknown or ignored human being (that is, someone who we do not respect). It is time to delete these last letters so that we are left with "brother"; every human being is a brother or a sister to every other human being. "Neither Jew nor gentile, neither man nor woman, neither master nor slave, for all of you are called upon to become children of God by adoption" (Gal 3:28).

DEDICATION OF THE STATUE OF MARIAM BEWARDI

There are many and varied celebrations with this conscious and implicit content: "Today, the Virgin comes to the cave to give birth to the Word that existed before the ages." What is missing from these celebrations is the festival or the celebration of the reception. For this reception, we invite you all, individually and collectively, your families, friends, and relatives, to join the teachers of Mar Elias Educational Institutions next Monday, the twenty-third of this month, in this church, where we will receive and crown the Christmas celebration. We receive the One born of Mary, "and He is our God before the ages." Immediately after the divine liturgy, we will walk together to the western part of the great square, where we receive and dedicate the statue of Saint Mariam Bewardi.

I am pleased to mention, in this context, that the person who carved this statue from our country's stones, two meters high, is a graduate of the Mar Elias Institutions. He got paid for his work, of course, but he created sacred work. Following the dedication of the statue, through prayer and chanting, we invite everyone to a modest reception. I remind you that the invitation for next Monday, December 23, 2019, is addressed to everyone; you are invited to crown the celebrations by receiving the Lord Jesus, born in the cave of Bethlehem, and on Monday, he is born again in our hearts in the Holy Eucharist. After the Mass, we will unveil the statue of Saint Mariam Bewardi, a daughter of Ibillin. It is a life-sized statue, one meter and seventy-five centimeters, made of hard stone cut from the vicinity of Bethlehem.

As we end our time together, I want, once again, to congratulate the inspiring choir, and I wish on behalf of you all continued activity and brilliance. You bring down heaven into the hearts of everyone who hears you wherever you go, wherever you visit, and you bring joy to the people. Best wishes for the new year. Christ is born, so receive him. Christ came from the heavens, so glorify him.

The ceremony ended with a feeling of reverence, contemplation, admiration, and love throughout the time we spent together.

JESUS' PRAYER IS THE PATH TO HEAVEN

That night I did not sleep. I kept recalling, repeating, and reviewing in my memory the Lord's Prayer. After meditating for a long time about this prayer which Jesus Christ taught us, I felt that I have integrated all the prayers of the entire world in this short prayer. I got up, excited to write down my contemplations. To summarize these, I understand that Jesus's prayer consists of three songs of praises and three requests or supplications, all directed to God who loves us as a divine Parent.

The three songs of praises are:

The Sermon on the Mount

Our Father who art in heaven

1) Hallowed be thy name.

2) Thy kingdom come,

3) thy will be done, on earth as it is in heaven.

I paused for a very long time at every praise, and I felt as if I were in front of an inexhaustible fountain. How great are your works, O Lord! They are all made wisely!

And the three supplications are:

Our Father who art in heaven

1) *Give us this day our daily bread.* Bread, as mentioned previously, is extracted from wheat, and wheat is a call to humanity, to respect pluralism, and to consider what is positive in that pluralism. The word for wheat is a compound of three letters. If we contemplate them, in this regard, we can read, "O our Father who are in heaven, give us wisdom, so that we can add Eid al-Adha to Christmas, and add both to the Festival of Lights (Hanukkah)." Thus, we take the moral lesson from the monotheistic religions and re-share them in order to make human society more humane for everyone.

2) *And forgive us our trespasses, as we forgive those who trespass against us.* The trespasses of human beings are the result of them falsifying their relationship with their brother and sister and their relationship with God the Creator, as well as their relationship with the near and distant universe. Our relationship with God directs us to relationships with other human beings. If we forgive them, the loving God will forgive us. If we do not forgive those who wronged us, our God will be reluctant to forgive us for when we disobeyed him and hurt our neighbors.

3) *And lead us not into temptation, but deliver us from evil.* We mention here the trials of Jesus Christ after he fasted for forty

days. "If you are the Son of God, command that the stone turn into bread, throw yourself from the top of the temple, bow your head before me, and I will give you these kingdoms that have been given to me. If you are a Christian, turn the other cheek to us."

But Christ did not succumb to any one of these trials; rather, he rejected them all. There was one and only way left before him for the salvation of humankind and for people to return to God. It was a way that he chose out of his extreme love: "there is no greater love than this, for a person to lay down his life as an offering for his loved ones" (John 15:13). This is the meaning of the cross, the meaning of pain, the strength of faith, and the steadfastness of love.

The justification for making all these praises and requests is this: "For yours, our Father who art in heaven, is the kingdom, the power, and the glory forever, Amen." This is a declaration of faith in God, and this is the justification for raising these prayers and requests to God since he has the glory, the power, and the reign.

I was contemplating these three supplications as if I was swimming in a large, deep sea, one in which dimensions are immeasurable and depths are unfathomable, and which encompasses all ports of life. As for the three songs of praise, they include all the songs of praise in the Old and New Testaments, as well as all the carols of the universe.

The supplications or requests are a condensed summary of all the requests and prayers in the New Testament, and I will try later to touch on some of their details. Suffice it to say for now that this is what the divine Teacher taught us: not to babble when we pray and to speak with words carefully chosen so that our prayers can be answered. Let our words be few and meaningful—that is, let your "Yes" be "Yes" and your "No" be "No!" Anything more than this is just a string of empty words.

It is now twelve o'clock at night. May creation revert to its original beauty, and into your hands, O God, I entrust my soul. How beautiful it is for a person to sleep when one's soul is immersed in the depth of God's love for humanity and creation. Nothing is more precious than Jesus Christ. Creation is a trust placed by the

Creator in the hands of every human being. God does not burden a soul beyond its capacity. All of these things are attainable, and they are the responsibility of every human being towards God, towards others, and towards nature as a whole. It is a responsibility for which we will be held accountable. The Requester (the One to whom we are accountable) is the trusting Giver. "What did you do with the talents I put in your hands to invest? Did you do something positive, or did you bury them, watching creation with a variety of different emotions and not seeing your mark after you left?" The Lord God gives great importance to our responsibility to be the light of the world and uses for this purpose the customs observed when Jesus was with us on earth. There is no doubt that he saw his Holy mother and saw Saint Joseph lighting the lamp every evening and placing it on the lampstand so that the people of the house could see the light. The lamp dispels the darkness, and he is not seen by anyone unless the light of the lamp is out in the open, not under a bowl where it will inevitably go out. Then darkness will prevail, and the people of the house will stumble. Place the lamp on the lampstand so that those present can see its light, and everyone can see what is in front of them and in which direction they walk. Otherwise, if the lamp does not illuminate the house, then stumbling of the people of the house is an inevitable danger, especially the young ones who will fall into the well inside the house.

Our house in Kafr Birim had a well in it from which we drew water. If someone fell inside it, he would inevitably drown. You are the light of the world, placed on the lampstand of society so that people can see your light, just like a city built on a mountain which one cannot ignore. There is no doubt that the Savior looked behind him and saw on Mount Canaan the city of Safad, and people could see it even from Haifa and Nazareth. It cannot be hidden. It is a marker for everyone who has eyes and can see. Thus, let your light shine before the people so that they may see your good deeds and glorify God who is in heaven. Let us understand that it is a curse when our light in front of the people is so bright that it blinds their eyes. The people see our light, and onlookers are dazzled; thus they only see you, the human, and praise you, mortals, and not the heavenly Parent. This is just like a butterfly so dazzled by light that it rushes towards it and gets burnt. Here we can enjoy the teachings of Jesus Christ and the miracles he performed, how he gave glory to God in everything he did and in everything in creation. He said to them: "How is it that you sought me? Did you not know that I must be in my Father's house?" (Luke 2:48–49). He continued, saying, "Do not think that I have come to abolish the law, but to fulfill it. Verily I say to you, heaven and earth will disappear, but not one letter of the law will disappear" (Matt 5:17–18). Whoever despises even the smallest commandment will be the least in the realm of heaven, and whoever respects it, teaches it, and lives it will be great in the realm of heaven.

Here, it is necessary to mention the Essenes community and their customs and traditions. They were known in history to be from the Qumran community near the Dead Sea. They left Jerusalem because evil was rampant there, and its inhabitants were the children of darkness. They left Jerusalem and returned to the desert to continue the faith of their ancestors by relying on God in the desert, where there is no helper but God Almighty. They respected the law, down to its smallest detail. It was their custom to copy the Holy Book (many of them were scribes), and after they had finished copying the book, they would give it to the proofreaders who would read the manuscript, and if they found a missing letter, dot, or word, they would consider the entire book incomplete. It was not permissible to correct it, because there was no authority for any person to correct or fix the word of God. It would not be permissible to use the book and then to burn it because the word of God could not be burned, nor was it permissible to dispose of it. They considered a manuscript missing even a single period to be dead. So, they would bury it with a funeral ceremony. They believed that divine providence dictated the document and that the son of the Ta'amari tribe from Jericho would discover all such buried manuscripts. It was in the late forties of the twentieth century that these documents were discovered.

Christ, glory be to him, continues the serious warning to his disciples, saying, "Unless your righteousness exceeds that of the Pharisees and scribes, you will not enter the kingdom of heaven" (Matt 5:20).

HE SPEAKS AS ONE WHO HAS AUTHORITY

After this announcement to the disciples, the Master, glory be to him, begins to describe the life of the Christian, to describe the Christian's position on the Old Testament, and to explain the distortions made by the scribes and Pharisees in their interpretations of the law. Jesus wanted to restore the truth and purity to the law. He warns against the falsifications that the teachers of the law introduced and through which they distorted the commandments of God. He spoke because he was the lawgiver and the guardian of the law.

We hear him as he spoke: "You have heard that it was said to the ancients: Do not kill, for whoever kills, deserves judgment. But I say to you: Your righteousness (justice) must be better than the righteousness (justice) of the Pharisees and the scribes, and I say to you that whoever says to his brother (or sister), 'You fool!' deserves the judgment of the law" (Matt 5:21–22).

And whoever says to his brother, "You are crazy" (in contempt) deserves the fire of hell. And you, disciple of Christ, if you go to the temple to make your offering, and there you remember that your brother (or sister) has something against you, or that you are indebted to them, leave your offering in the temple and first go and make peace with your brother or sister and then come and make your offering. We cannot honor God, whom we do not see, and despise our brother or sister, whom we do see.

You, the disciple of Christ, make amends with your brother and sister as long as you are with them on the road, lest they hand you over to the governor, who will condemn you and throw you in prison. Truly I tell you: you will not get out of prison until you pay the last penny you owe.

The divine Teacher, the Master of the law and the *Nomos*, adds: "You have heard that it was said, 'You shall not commit adultery.' But I say to you, everyone who looks at a woman in lust has committed adultery in his heart" (Matt 5:27–28). Adultery begins in the heart. The adulterer is the one who stands naked before false gods. Therefore, if your eye makes you doubt, gouge them out; for it is better for you to enter the kingdom as a one-eyed person than for your whole body to be thrown into hell. And if your right hand causes you trouble, cut it off and throw it away from you. It is better for you to enter the kingdom as a one-armed person than for your whole body to be cast into hell.

"You have heard that it was said: 'Whoever wants to divorce his wife must give her a certificate of divorce, then divorce her.' But I say to you: Anyone who divorces his wife, except for sexual immorality, makes her the victim of adultery, and anyone who marries a divorced woman commits adultery and disobeys the law. What God has joined together, let no one separate" (Matt 5:31–32). It is certain that the Master, glory be to him, had before him the image of Herod, who fell in love with the wife of his brother Philip, so he killed his brother and married his wife. John the Baptist constantly rebuked Herod because he did not have the right to take his brother's wife as his own wife, and so Herod put John in prison and was afraid of him. But in submission to the desire of the same woman, Herodias, John was beheaded. Jesus's public message then began. You have heard that it was said to the ancients, "Do not break your oath" (Matt 5:31).

At the end of this contemplation, we are still at the beginning of the road, and from here, we begin again to give ourselves to loving others and joining with God in creating a more just and peaceful world. The great teachings of the Sermon on the Mount are my "credentials," and they are what has guided me across the years of my life. They continue to express the call of God to continue my life work.

The Sermon on the Mount

Questions for Personal Reflection and Study Groups

Drawing upon the wisdom and guidance from the Sermon on the Mount, Matt 5–7, how might you answer or deal with the following questions?

1. On a scale of 1–10, with 10 being most extreme, what is the level of your fears and anxiety in your day-to-day life? And what is your level of peace and contentment?

2. What are the resources you have for dealing with anger, fear, and anxiety? How do you find joy and deep happiness?

3. In what ways does the Christian faith give you guidance and a good measure of purpose and security? Or does it?

4. What parts of the Sermon on the Mount do you find most valuable? The Lord's Prayer? the Beatitudes? the golden rule? other wisdom sayings? What guidance on ethical questions does the Sermon on the Mount give you?

5. Do you have a life-giving community that gives you a sense of belonging, of having friends who accept and support you? Would they help you if you were to be in great need with an illness, a fundamental shift in your work, or the loss of a foundational relationship such as a marriage partner?

6. How would you describe the quality of your friendships, and do you wish for more friendships that are filled with care and understanding?

7. How would you describe the meaning of your life? Do you wish for more clarity about the meaning and value of your life?

8. How would you describe your way of dealing with really difficult problems, such as the loss of a relationship or a job, or the lack of financial resources to take good care of your life?

9. If you had two wishes, with the promise that you would receive what you want, what would they be?

10. In what ways do the life and teaching of Jesus give you guidance and comfort? If not from Jesus, from whom might you find a good way to live, giving you deep happiness?

Bibliography and Background Reading[1]

Augustine. *Confessions.* Translated by R. S. Pine-Coffin. London: Penguin Classics, 1961.
Allison, Dale C. *Constructing Jesus: Memory, Imagination, and History.* Grand Rapids: Baker Academic, 2010.
Bailey, Kenneth E. *Jesus Through Middle Eastern Eyes: Cultural Studies in the Gospels.* Downers Grove, IL: IVP Academic, 2008.
Borg, Marcus J. *Jesus: Uncovering the Life, Teachings, and Relevance of a Religious Revolutionary.* New York: HarperOne, 2006.
Bornkamm, Gunther. *Jesus of Nazareth.* Reprint, New York: Harper, 1960.
Bourgeault, Cynthia. *The Wisdom Jesus: Transforming Heart and Mind—A New Perspective on Christ and His Message.* Boston: Shambhala, 2008.
Connick, C. Milo. *Jesus: The Man, The Mission, and the Message.* 2nd ed. Englewood Cliffs, NJ: Prentice Hall, 1974.
Crossan, John Dominic. *Jesus: A Revolutionary Biography.* New York: HarperCollins, 1993.
Echegaray, Hugo. *The Practice of Jesus.* Maryknoll, NY: Orbis, 1984.
Edersheim, Alfred. *The Life and Times of Jesus the Messiah.* 2 vols. London: Longmans, Green and Co., 1950.
Ferguson, Duncan S. *The Radical Invitation of Jesus.* Eugene, OR: Wipf & Stock, 2019.

---

1. Note: There are literally thousands—perhaps millions—of books about Jesus, and they range from very scholarly to quite popular, from an expressed desire to claim Jesus for one's own point of view to a commitment to write a historical account without bias, and—sadly for the reader—to use the name of Jesus to justify the ways of a dangerous cultic leader. One needs to use some care in selecting books about Jesus. In consultation with the author, Abuna Elias Chacour, I, Duncan Ferguson, serving as an editor, have suggested a few books with different ways of helping us understand Jesus. They are written with careful scholarship and in a way which will assist readers within the Christian church to find guidance, as well as to those with a deep desire to learn about this one whose life and teaching may be the most influential of anyone who ever lived.

Bibliography and Background Reading

———. *The Radical Teaching of Jesus.* Eugene, OR: Wipf & Stock, 2016.
Fredriksen, Paula. *Jesus of Nazareth: King of the Jews.* New York: Random House, 1999.
Horsley, Richard A. *Jesus: and the Politics of Roman Palestine.* Reprint, Eugene, OR: Cascade, 2021.
Meier, John P. *A Marginal Jew: Rethinking the Historical Jesus.* 4 vols. New York: Doubleday, 1991–2009.
Moltmann, Jurgen. *Jesus Christ for Today's World.* Minneapolis: Fortress, 1994.
Murry, Frederick J. *The Religious World of Jesus.* Nashville: Abingdon, 1991.
Phillips, J. B. *Your God Is Too Small: A Guide for Believers and Skeptics Alike.* Reprint, New York: Touchstone, 2004.
Powell, Mark Allen. *Jesus as a Figure in History.* Louisville: Westminster John Knox, 1998.
Sanders, E. P. *The Historical Figure of Jesus*, 1991.
Schweitzer, Albert. *The Quest for the Historical Jesus: A Critical Study of Its Progress from Reimarus to Wrede.* Translated by W. Montgomery. Reprint, Greenwood, WI: Suzeteo, 2011.
Wright, N. T. *Jesus and the Victory of God.* Minneapolis: Fortress, 1996.

www.ingramcontent.com/pod-product-compliance
Lightning Source LLC
Chambersburg PA
CBHW070508090426
42735CB00012B/2696